# WEST HAM'S

**WEST HAM UNITED**

# 30 MEMORABLE MATCHES

# WEST HAM'S
# 30 MEMORABLE MATCHES

## PHILIP STEVENS

DB PUBLISHING

# ACKNOWLEDGEMENTS

Debbie Silver at West Ham
Steve Marsh at www.theyflysohigh
Stuart Allen
Graeme Howlett at www.kumb
Mirrorpix.

First published in Great Britain in 2011 by The Derby Books Publishing Company Limited, 3 The Parker Centre, Derby, DE21 4SZ.

ISBN 978-1-85983-871-6
Printed and bound by Melita Press, Malta.

# CONTENTS

# INTRODUCTION

The 30 matches described here recreate the special moments of a club with some of the most devoted and proud supporters in football. The matches included reflect the triumphs and disasters in the long history of West Ham United FC. Some recall thumping victories, where individual players rose gloriously to the occasion, and others remind us of the brittle fragility of West Ham's commitment to attacking football. Football matches are memorable for goals, goalmouth incidents and end-to-end free-flowing football, or are simply special occasions, like the White Horse Cup Final of 1923.

The primary aim of this book is to bring to life key matches in the history of one of Britain's most cherished football clubs. Players such as Moore, Hurst and Peters, the Liverpool Cup Final of 2006 – said to be the greatest of the modern era – Ron Greenwood's football academy and the white-hot atmosphere of European nights at Upton Park are all treasured memories of the West Ham faithful.

The strong family tradition, a reputation for surging attacking football and hair-tingling moments when the excitement at Upton Park mounts to an almost unbearable level, are all part of being a Hammers supporter, as are the high and lows of promotion and relegation. Every season has produced memorable moments.

The stories surrounding these games have been compiled through research from old newspapers, from talking to former players and older supporters, and by delving into some of the many books written about the club and its history. It has been a privilege to bring together the special memories of a football club so rich in tradition.

I have my own recollections of supporting the Hammers, which go back to the early 1960s, and I can still see a young Bobby Moore strolling out for his first home game, but the club dates from the late 19th century, and the book begins with a couple of matches involving the original Irons pioneers. I hope all West Ham fans and football lovers in general will enjoy reading of the elation, despair, celebration and heartbreak in the fortunes of the claret and blue pride of East London.

# 1.

# THAMES IRONWORKS FC

# V BARKING

## CHARITY CUP FINAL       21 MARCH 1896

*In the summer of 1895, when the clanging of 'hammers' was heard on the banks of Father Thames and the great warships were rearing their heads above the Victoria Dock Road, a few enthusiasts, with a love of football...were talking about the formation of a club for the workers of the Thames Ironworks Ltd.*

**Syd King, Thames Irons player and West Ham United Manager 1902–32**

Thames Ironworks FC resigned from the Southern League in 1900, and the club was officially wound up in July of that year. Almost immediately the club reformed under the name of West Ham United and accepted the resulting vacant Southern League place. In 1904 the new club moved to its present ground at Upton Park. These facts conceal a rich and fascinating history of one of England's most iconic football clubs.

Every West Ham fan understands and respects the origins of the club, which explains why they are called 'the Hammers' and why, to the bemusement of visiting fans, the chant 'Come on, you Irons' continues. The Upton Park faithful are proud that their club originated from the streets, factories and dockyards of their own neighbourhoods. They are aware that generations of their families going back over 100 years lived and worked in the area and supported their club. It is important that a book about the most memorable matches of the Hammers should recognise this history, and this particular match represents a key stage in the emerging tale of West Ham United FC.

The Thames Ironworks and Shipbuilding Co. Ltd employed 6,000 people in East London. At its yards in Blackwall and Canning Town, the company was at the forefront of new engineering methods and in 1850 built the HMS Warrior, the world's first iron warship. The firm also provided the linings for the Blackwall Tunnel, built ships for the Royal Navy and was a vital part of the East End economy in the late 19th century.

The company was bought by Frank Hills in 1880 before he retired and handed it over to his son, Arnold. The Hills were a Christian family, and young Arnold was a patrician employer determined to keep his workers on the straight and narrow. Unlike many 19th century entrepreneurs, Arnold Hill lived close by his yard down in East India Dock Road and cared passionately about the welfare of his men, encouraging many of them to take the pledge. But he was no fool, and he realised that preaching alone would not change anything. Hills had played football for the University of Cambridge and knew the game was spreading rapidly across the country in working-class areas. This inspired him to form the Thames Ironworks FC – initially, perhaps, to keep his workers out of the pub. Probably closer to the truth was that Hills had been involved in a bitter industrial dispute at the firm and was keen to improve relations with his men. He wrote in the Thames Ironworks Gazette that he wanted to 'wipe away the bitterness left by the recent strike'.

In a renewed spirit of cooperation, his article invited workers to join a new football club. Hills must have been delighted when over 50 men signed up for the training sessions on Tuesday and Thursday nights at the gas-lit Trinity Church Hall in the Barking Road. The sessions were conducted in a military style, with long runs along the Beckton Road and strenuous physical training. It was clear that the club had serious intentions from the beginning.

Thames Ironworks FC, partly subsidised by the company, quickly took off, and within a few weeks the committee were urgently seeking fixtures for its two teams. The first match, a friendly against Royal Ordnance on 7 September 1895, ended in a 1–1 draw, and Thames Ironworks FC was on its way.

Hills' attempt to offer organised sport and leisure opportunities for his workers was part of a much wider trend in industry. East End companies like Tate & Lyle and Bryant & May also provided sporting and leisure activities for their employees and established playing fields and social clubs right across East London. They were part of the highly successful development of factory football over the next 75 years.

In 1897, buoyed by the success of his initiative, Hills acquired a new stadium for the princely sum of £20,000,  following short spells at Hermit Road and Browning Road. The Memorial Ground was to be Thames's new home for the next seven years. The new stadium had a capacity of 17,000 and accommodated a range of sports, including athletics and cycling as well as football. With such an excellent facility it became clear that the club needed to attract paying spectators.

Further friendly matches, including a night game against the mighty West Bromwich Albion, all of which attracted decent crowds, convinced committee members that local people would pay to watch their new team play. Attendances varied, but a fixture against Tottenham or Millwall would often attract crowds of 10,000 or more paying spectators. To enable his employees to get to the games, Hills even had a crude set of lights set up so that matches could be played in the evenings.

In 1896 an application by the club to join the London League was accepted, despite East and West Ham being in Essex at the time. In their first season in senior amateur football, Thames finished runners-up, and in 1897–98 they confirmed their huge promise by winning the League, following an away win at the Grenadier Guards on the last day of the season. Thames were later promoted to the Southern League, becoming a professional club for the first time. As a professional outfit they were able to strengthen the side by recruiting good players from the likes of Millwall, Manchester City and former-London League rivals, the Grenadier Guards. The club had made rapid progress in a very short time, and was about to win their first trophy.

Looking at the origins of the Hammers, one match stands out – Thames Ironworks versus Barking in the West Ham Charity Cup Final of 1896. The match was played at the Old Spotted Dog ground, home to Clapton FC, and was confirmation, thanks to the hard work of Arnold Hills, local volunteers and the players, that the club was now established. Thames had lost in the Final of the same competition the previous season, and the players were determined not to fail a second time. The team was full of confidence, having beaten their arch-rivals, St Luke's from Beckton, in a tough semi-final. In addition, Thames had enjoyed a successful season, having won 30 of their 46 games. The talented team included Essex cricketer John Wood and the promising 17-year-old William Barnes. A local poet was so inspired by his team reaching a Cup Final that he wrote the following lines:

On Monday you meet Barking,
And you'll win the cup I think,
So on Monday the Iron expects
Out of it to have drink.

The 1896 Final was an extremely close encounter between local rivals, and it required two replays to settle the tie. The first match, on the 21 March, ended in a hard-fought 2–2 draw, with Johnny Stewart and skipper Robert Stevenson scoring for the Irons. It was an exciting game – end-to-end action, watched by an excitable and noisy crowd pressed up against the ropes surrounding the pitch. The teams reassembled at the Old Spotted Dog a week later and ground out an uneventful 0-0 draw, about which the less said the better.

The second replay was held on a Monday evening three weeks later at St Luke's ground in Becton. Cheered on by a crowd of 3,000 people, mostly from Canning Town, Thomas Freeman and George Sage missed early chances to put the Irons ahead. After 20 minutes, a serious injury to Langford reduced Barking to 10 men as no substitutes allowed in the 19th century, even in Cup Finals. The Irons where quick to take advantage of the extra man, and winger Johnny Stewart continued to cause problems for the Barking defence with his direct running and nimble footwork. With Thames well on top, Freeman picked up a painful knock, and both sides were reduced to 10 men. But just as Barking began to get back into the game, Thames scored.

As the minutes ticked by, William Chamberlain won a corner with a deflected shot. With excitement mounting, George Sage took the kick and teenager Barnes was the first to react, firing a low shot into the corner of the Barking net to the delight of most of the crowd. Barking pressed hard for an equaliser in the dying minutes, but the Irons hung on to win their first-ever Cup competition.

The Thames teams for the three matches consisted of French, Graham, Woods, Hickman, Chamberlain, Sage, Faram, Chapman, Stewart, Freeman, Stevenson and Barnes.Originally a Thames player, goalscorer Billy Barnes played in the Final as a guest player from South West Ham. He came into the side due to injuries to several key players in the two previous games. Barnes contribution in the second replay was to prove decisive. A gifted, left-sided forward, Barnes had a long and distinguished professional career with Sheffield United, Queen's Park Rangers, Luton and West Ham. It is worth remembering that players of the day played with a heavy leather ball, wore huge leather boots and shinpads were often just a folded magazine stuffed down the socks. In wet conditions both ball and boots were soon caked in thick mud, negating the skills of the better players. But on this sunny evening young Barnes was in his element. He was the youngest player ever to appear in the Thames first team, and he entered West Ham folklore with his goal that day.

Compared to today's extravagant post-match carousing, the players celebrated well, but modestly. Following the game they headed down to the Trinity School Rooms in the Barking Road, where they were welcomed by members of the committee. The Cup was filled with beer and continually passed among a group of very happy and vocal young footballers.

To mark the occasion, the club held an official reception at Canning Town Public Hall, where the players were presented with their medals by Arnold Hills. Like most award ceremonies of the time, the event was a formal dinner and dance, with players and their partners appropriately clad in their Sunday best.

The West Ham Charity Cup raised considerable sums for local good causes, and the organising committee of 1895–96 must have been delighted with the proceeds raised from three Cup Finals in one year. Thames had every reason to be proud of winning the trophy in its inaugural season.

The 1896 Final was an important stage on the long journey of the Thames Ironworks and West Ham United partnership. During the 20th century West Ham became known as a Cup side, their elegant, classical passing game and brittle defence not built to withstand the rigours of a long winter League Championship. The West Ham Charity Cup was to prove the first of several Cup triumphs in the joint history of the clubs.

In the early days Thames did have some League success. The club's best performances were saved for the Southern League, the most prestigious in the south of England, which included Tottenham Hotspur, Millwall and Fulham. Within a very short period Thames showed they had had truly arrived in the senior ranks of English football by winning promotion to the First Division. During the club's spell in the Southern League, Thames recorded wins against Spurs, Fulham and Southampton, a remarkable achievement and a tribute to Arnold Hill, his secretary, Francis Payne, and the committee members, all of whom were volunteers.

In 1900, the year the club was elected to the Southern League, Thames decided to become a limited company in their own right and severed their connections with the parent company. At this time the firm ran into difficulties as it struggled to compete with the shipyards in the north of England. In 1911 the Blackwall yard launched the 22,500 ton Thunderer, the last ship ever to be constructed on the Thames.

A further reason for the split was that Hills, ever the idealist, wanted to keep the rule, which meant that only employees of the firm could play for the club. But as Thames became more successful and the committee more ambitious, the local amateur footballers who served the club so well were now longer good enough for the next stage of development. Thames needed new and better players to compete in the Southern League than were available in the factory. The split was inevitable.

In due course, Thames Ironworks FC, now independent, changed their name to West Ham United and moved to their new home, Upton Park. The Hammers originally played in the Southern League before achieving Football League status in 1919. There is a story that the claret and blue colours adopted by West Ham were selected because the father of Thames legend Charlie Dove, a professional sprinter, won a race against a couple of Aston Villa players. The 'payment' for his successful bet was a set of Villa claret and blue shirts, stolen from the club by one of the players. It is likely that this tale is more legend than fact and that the colours do originate from Hill's Ironworks livery, but the story has become part of Hammers folklore.

The Thames's founder, Arnold Hill, died in 1927, but his legacy lives on in East London today. His company eventually folded, unable to withstand the intense competition from northern shipbuilders, who had coal mines, steel yards and iron foundries on their doorstep. Hill's works eventually closed, failing to provide the jobs he knew local people needed and that he was desperate to provide for them. But the founder of Thames played a significant part in the formation of West Ham United by extending the lease on the Memorial Ground to the new club. He continued to support the Hammers and held no grudges about the loss of his beloved Thames Ironworks FC.

As a professional football club, West Ham United is inextricably linked to its local history. The cross-hammers on the club's official crest ensure its local and industrial roots are not forgotten. The fans' chant of 'Come on, you Irons' is a constant reminder of a proud shipbuilding past and a permanent attachment to the River Thames.

# 2.

# WEST HAM UNITED

# V BOLTON WANDERERS

## FA CUP FINAL                    28 APRIL 1923

West Ham United, formerly Thames Ironworks, spent their first 15 years playing with moderate success in the Southern and Western Leagues. But the club was ambitious and in 1919 eventually gained entry to the Second Division of the Football League. Four years later, managed by Syd King and assistant Charlie Paynter, they won promotion to the First Division and reached the Final of the FA Cup for the first time.

Arnold Hills would have been proud of his old club. He may not have approved of the new climate of professionalism in the English game, but he would have loved the fact that West Ham now represented the whole of East London rather than just an area around Blackwall and Canning Town.

The 1923 Cup Final, or, as it was more quaintly known at the time, The Football Association English Cup Competition – Final Tie, was the first to be played at the new Empire Stadium at Wembley. The architects and McAlpine, the construction company, were determined that the stadium that would have no structural defects. They wanted no repeat of the 1920 Ibrox disaster, when a stand collapsed, tragically killing 20 spectators. The new stadium was completed in 300 working days at a total cost of £750,000. The construction team used 25,000 tons of concrete, 1,500 tons of steel, and over a million rivets. Cup Finals continued to be played at the old ground until the year 2000.

The FA took unusual steps to ensure the terracing was safe. A week before the Final was due to be played, a battalion of infantry marked time on the terraces for 15 minutes to test that they were strong enough to take the weight of the capacity crowd of 125,000. It was original, if not very scientific.

The new stadium was built on the site of Wembley Park, the venue for the British Empire Exhibition. It was originally meant to be pulled down after the Exhibition,

*West Ham in April 1923, on the verge of their historic Wembley appearance. Back row (left to right): E.S.King (manager), Henderson, Bishop, Kay, Hufton, Young, Tresadern, C.Paynter (trainer). Front row: Richards, Brown, Watson, Moore, Ruffell.*

*West Ham supporters arrive at Wembley for the 1923 FA Cup Final, unaware that they are about to witness – or did they? – one of the most famous games in the history of football. Note the large 'hammer'. Today it would be an inflatable.*

but its famous Twin Towers and iconic 39 steps to the Royal Box saved the new home of football from demolition. Imagine the excitement at the time – a brand new national stadium with its first Cup Final, a London team at Wembley, and King George V in attendance to present the trophy to the winning team.

Remarkably, despite the enormity of the occasion, the match was not all-ticket. To be fair to the FA, nobody could have predicted the chaotic scenes that occurred on that sunny Saturday afternoon in April 1923. A crowd estimated anywhere between 200,000 and 300,000 poured into the new stadium from all parts of the country. The terraces simply could not accommodate the volume of people, and thousands of angry fans were forced onto the perimeter of the pitch. As kick-off approached, hundreds of people flooded onto the playing surface itself. The Times's aerial photographs of the scenes show the true extent of the confusion and chaos down on the pitch.

At 1.00pm, with so many people in the ground, the stadium authorities decided to close the gates. Eye-witness accounts reveal that turnstile operators fled in the chaos, leaving hundreds of people without tickets free to climb over the turnstiles into the ground. Police were powerless to stop the tide of people entering the stadium.

The Bolton team were forced to abandon their team coach several miles from the ground and fought their way through Wembley on foot. FA officials were acutely aware that the King was in the ground and were desperate to get the game started, but they decided to delay the kick-off for 45 minutes while police and officials attempted to restore some order. Mounted police were brought in to clear the pitch so the game could begin.

*More mounted officers attempt to hold the Wembley crowd in check.*

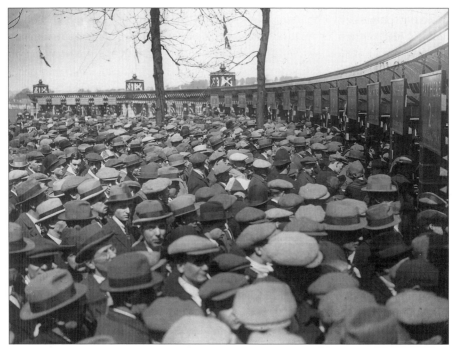

*Crowds swarm towards the Wembley turnstiles for the 1923 Cup Final. Interest in the game took the authorities by surprise, leading to some of the most remarkable scenes ever seen at a football match.*

*PC Storey on his white horse, Billie, attempts to push back the crowd. Ever since the game has been known as 'the White Horse Final'. Of course there were other mounted policeman doing an equally sterling job, but Billie stood out.*

At this point, and in the midst of the pandemonium preceding the match, an unlikely hero emerged. PC George Scorey and Billy, his calm and courageous white horse, led the police efforts to clear the crowd. From that day the 1923 Cup Final was written in football folklore as the White Horse Final. PC Scorey was later offered the freedom of Wembley Stadium, but he was not a football fan and chose to stay at home and tend his garden. In a public poll to name the new footbridge at the revamped stadium, The White Horse Bridge was the popular choice.

As a result of the brave efforts of the policeman and his horse, the match eventually got under way, and there were some wonderful players on view that day. West Ham manager Syd King must have approached the game with confidence, having exciting attacking players like centre-forward Vic Watson and winger Jimmy Ruffell in his team. His opposite number, Charles Foweraker, had his own reason to be hopeful. His side included one of the most dangerous forwards in the country in the exciting David Jack.

Meanwhile, in the brand-new Wembley dressing rooms, the players of Bolton and West Ham prepared to face the disorderly scenes out on the field above them. Bolton's route to the Final had been relatively smooth. The Wanderers, who had finished the season in 13th place in the First Division, had beaten Sheffield United 1–0 in a tight semi-final encounter at Old Trafford. The match was played in front of a crowd of 72,000, a new record for an FA Cup semi-final.

For the Hammers the 1922–23 season could hardly have been more dramatic. Having secured promotion to the top flight by the by the narrowest of margins, they now found themselves in the FA Cup Final at Wembley. In truth, West Ham had a rather fortunate Cup run. All five of the teams they faced were from the Second Division or lower, which made the Londoners the first club to reach the FA Cup final without facing opposition from the top division. It took the East Londoners three games to defeat Southampton in the fourth round, but they reached the Final with a thumping 5–2 win over Derby County in the semi-final at Stamford Bridge. Hopes were flying high in the East End. The East Ham Echo wrote on 4 May:

**West Ham United, of whose fine performances on the football field everybody is talking about...are confidently being named as certain winners of the English Cup in the first Final at the great new stadium at Wembley.**

The club were enjoying one of the best seasons in their history, but, as so often happens in Cup Finals, the favourites were made to struggle. The Hammers had a very difficult day indeed.

As the dressing room clocks approached 3.00pm, all both sets of players wanted to do was get the match started. Somehow, they were able to leave the tunnel and reach the pitch in safety. By this time the crowd had calmed and begun assisting with a clear-up operation, and at last the referee was able to blow his whistle to signal the start of the game. With spectators 10-deep around the touchline, however, the players could hardly be expected to produce a nail-biting match full of free-

*West Ham players look perplexed as the match is delayed while the mammoth task of clearing the pitch gets under way*

*Some fans took a slightly safer route into the stadium where they probably found themselves still unable to see the action.*

*But this fan seems absolutely intent on getting in to see the 1923 Cup Final, even if it means risking life and limb.*

flowing football. Referee Asson had an impossible job as he tried to get through the 90 minutes. At times he could not apply the rules as strictly as he would have liked. Players had no room to run up for corners and goal-kicks, and the ball bounced off spectators back into play, on one occasion leading to a goal being scored. The referee could have lost control at any moment. These were not the conditions for a classic FA Cup Final, and one spectator described the scenes as 'a bloody shambles'. Others put it more strongly.

Bolton's defensive dour and defensive style contrasted sharply with the fast, attacking football for which the Hammers were becoming renowned. Both teams adopted the old-style system of two full-backs, a centre-half, two-half-backs, and five forwards. The Londoners game-plan was to get the ball out quickly to their two speedy wingers, Jimmy Ruffell and Dick Richards, and try to turn the Bolton defence. However, Bolton's rearguard were superbly organised and easily contained the early threat from the Hammers' forwards. Then the inevitable happened as the crowd began to encroach onto the pitch, narrowing the width of the playing area. After just a few minutes, the West Ham full-back, Jack Tresaden, got entangled in a group of fans on the touchline after taking a throw-in. Bolton took the throw quickly while Tresaden was still in the crowd. With the Hammer's defence one man short, David Jack was put through on goal, and the centre-forward hammered his shot high into the net, allegedly knocking out a spectator positioned directly behind the goal.

The early lead relaxed the northerners and they began to control the pace of the game. Just before the interval, play was stopped for a short time as the crowd made one of their regular incursions onto the pitch. When the game resumed Bolton continued to profit from their negative tactics, designed to disrupt the Hammers' passing game. They reached half-time with their one-goal lead intact. Bolton's game-plan had worked perfectly to the extent that the Hammers were never allowed

*David Jack scores the historic first Wembley goal for Bolton Wanderers.*

to get into the first half. With hundreds of excited fans lining the touchline, both sets of players chose to remain on the pitch rather than try to fight their way to their dressing rooms.

Police managed to quieten the crowd so the match could resume after the interval. Urged on by their loyal fans, West Ham began the second half brightly. But the staunch Bolton defence continued to stifle the Hammers' best attacking efforts as settled into their dull routine. Perhaps the threatening atmosphere in the stadium favoured a dour defensive rearguard, rather than the sparkling attacking display expected from the West Ham academy of football. The pitch deteriorated under the feet of hundreds of fans, which made it difficult for the Hammers to play their usual passing game.

West Ham did have their chances, but Bolton destroyed what lingering hopes their fans had when Jack Smith scored for his side in the 53rd minute. The goal was highly controversial because the West Ham defence claimed Smith's mis-hit shot had failed to cross the line and had rebounded into play after hitting the foot of a post. But the referee gave the goal, insisting that the ball did not hit the post but was deflected back into play by a spectator standing behind the net.

West Ham's frustration with the officials increased as the spectators began to influence the ebb and flow of the match. The Irons' players complained long and hard to the referee about crowd interference, but Mr Asson, keen to finish the match, refused to listen. George Kay, the Hammers' skipper, pleaded with Asson to abandon the match, but his opposite number, Joe Smith, was happy to continue.

Who could blame him, with his side 2–0 ahead with just 20 minutes left of the FA Cup Final? All West Ham's protest fell on deaf ears, and, in any case, the crowd began to quieten and drift away in the last 15 minutes as they sensed an inevitable Bolton victory.

*This time Jack is beaten to the ball by the West Ham defence.*

The referee blew the final whistle, and Bolton fans began their celebrations. Joe Smith gleefully received the Cup from King George. What a day for the Second Division club and its supporters.

The losers were inconsolable. After what became a memorable match for all the wrong reasons, the legendary Hammers' trainer, Charlie Paynter, expressed his club's bitter disappointment in graphic style:

**It was that white horse thumping its big feet into the pitch that made it hopeless. Our wingers were tumbling all over the place, tripping up in great ruts and holes.**

Paynter had a point. The Londoners were prevented from gracing the occasion with their normal attacking game. But credit to Bolton for sticking to their game-plan and staying resolute. It was a long time before the Hammers were to have another chance to lift the coveted trophy.

The Stratford Express, great supporters of the Hammers, got it about right:

There was every prospect, under normal conditions, of witnessing one of the finest exhibitions ever seen in a final for the FA Cup, but in the circumstances neither side showed its best form. Bolton won because they more nearly approached their more usual form than West Ham did. (30 April 1923)

In truth, the result of the match hardly seemed to matter. The FA authorities had botched what should have been one of the greatest occasions in the history of English

*Heads high in the Bolton defence as West Ham mount an attack.*

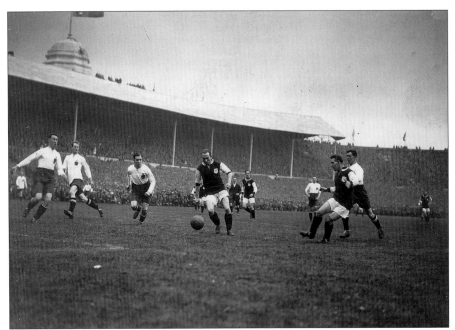

*Billy Moore takes a pass from Jimmy Ruffell and the Hammers press again.*

football – the first FA Cup Final at Wembley. It was a miracle that nobody died, although over 900 people were injured, 22 seriously, including two police officers.

Following the 1923 debacle, Cup Finals became all-ticket. New turnstiles were introduced and the terraces divided into sections each with their own entrance. Much later, spectators were segregated. Over the next 50 years the British public forgot 1923 and became hugely fond of their national stadium. But the FA shamefully neglected to maintain and modernise the jewel in the crown of English football. As the years passed, Wembley Stadium was allowed to go into slow decline and eventually had to be replaced, at a huge cost to the nation.

The White Horse match finances seem miserly when compared with the riches in football today. In 1923 the gate receipts were a £27,776, with a miserly £6,000 going to each of the finalists, though it is doubtful that the players considered financial reward on that famous day. Immediately after the match, both teams attended a dinner at which Lloyd George praised the behaviour of the police and the good nature of the crowd.

Bolton went home to a hero's civic reception, while the Hammers took the short journey back to East London to ponder what might have been. Both sets of players received gold medals to mark the occasion, a thoughtful gesture but not one that would have consoled the Hammers' team. The medal presented to the West Ham captain, George Kay, was sold at auction in 2005 for £4,560. The club's directors declined to appeal for the match to be replayed. They did have legitimate grounds, but with some dignity they took the view that they were beaten by a better team on the day.

The Home Secretary declined calls for a public enquiry into the events of the day and praised the police and stadium authorities for their good work. Both were ordered to draw up plans to prevent such a disaster ever happening again. But the controversy surrounding the events of the 1923 Final persisted. Some, as always, were quick to blame the fans. On the 30 April The Times claimed the gates were rushed by latecomers who failed to distribute themselves as evenly as they might have done on the standing terraces. The truth was that the FA failed to anticipate the enormous interest in the match and had little experience in handling events of this size. They failed to give serious consideration to appropriate ticket allocation and the safe movement of fans in and around the stadium. The Daily Mail described the stewarding as useless and stated that stadium officials seemed to know nothing. Fans were not directed to any specific area, and the tiers in the lower half of the stadium filled up much quicker than those higher up.

There is little doubt that the police acted sensibly and bravely, but the awful circumstances of the White Horse Final could have been avoided by more careful and thorough planning by the FA.

Typically, during the debate about the match in the House of Commons, Oswald Mosley, the right-wing Nazi-sympathising MP, described the fans that day as hooligans, a term used repeatedly, if undeservedly, ever since.

**Final score: West Ham United 0 Bolton Wanderers 2**

West Ham United: Hufton, Henderson, Young, Bishop, Kay (captain), Tresarden, Richards, Brown, Watson, Moore, Ruffell.

# 3.

# WEST HAM UNITED

# V CLAPTON ORIENT

## FOOTBALL LEAGUE DIVISION TWO    1922–23

In 1923 West Ham reached the FA Cup Final for the first time, but unfortunately for Hammers fans, Bolton were the better side on the day. The Wembley defeat was hard to take because the Londoners were strongly fancied to win. But despite this setback, the 1922–23 season was, in some respects, one of the most important in the club's history. If the White Horse Final lingers longer in the memory, as East London football historian Colm Kerrigan reminds us, promotion to Division One of the Football League was perhaps the more significant achievement.

Following promotion to the top flight, the club became a major force in English football and stayed in Division One for the next ten seasons. Over the years, the passionate followers of West Ham have suffered the disappointment of relegation and the odd humiliation in the FA Cup, but since 1923 the club has become established as one of the the top clubs in English football and has welcomed some of Europe's premier teams to Upton Park – not bad for a side that, in the early 20th century, was a works' team in the London League.

One of the reasons for West Ham's success in the formative years was the sheer popularity of football in the East End, described by Kerrigan as 'a hotbed of football'. Local leagues were being formed in the area, and senior amateur football was on the increase due in part to the success of the FA Amateur Cup. Many of the promising local youngsters found their way to Upton Park. This increase in participation required additional playing areas, and local councils and the Epping Forest Corporation worked hard to ensure that all local clubs had somewhere to play. Hackney Marshes, Wanstead Flats, Beckton Park, and West Ham Park were just a few of the grounds made available for local league football in the early part of the 19th century. Oxford and Cambridge universities helped to set up sports centres at Fairbairn House, Eton Mission and the Docklands

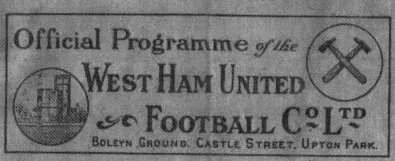

# Official Programme *of the*
## WEST HAM UNITED
### *&* FOOTBALL Co Ltd
#### BOLEYN GROUND, CASTLE STREET, UPTON PARK.

No. 16   Match No. 16     Nov. 18th, 1922     Price 2d.

*CLAPTON ORIENT*

## NOTES

THE value of goal-scoring forwards to us at the moment cannot be fully estimated. When one sees, week after week, chance after chance being frittered away by indecision, hesitation, and lack of accuracy in direction (and these failings were again evident in the match against Leeds last Saturday) one realises how much goal-scoring forwards would be appreciated.

Jack Tresadern was so disgusted with his forwards' efforts, that he had a try, but although his intentions were good, he fared no better with his efforts than the men in front of him.

Leeds United are not the team to stand any ceremony, but we have nothing particularly to find fault with in their go-ahead bustling methods.

Our visitors from Homerton to-day are very welcome, and they will endeavour to do better than when they visited us in the Second Round of the London Cup, but their recent performance of drawing with the Manchester United team was very creditable. They (like ourselves) need points, therefore the game to-day is bound to be a thrilling one, and someone is sure to be disappointed this evening. It may be the "Hammers" or it may be the "Orientals," but let us hope that the game will be a sporting one.

Opportunity was taken on Thursday to try George Carter at centre-forward (which was his original position) and W. Charlton at out-side right, the latter re-appearing after six weeks' absence.

*The West Ham programme from 18 November 1922.*

Settlements, which encouraged young people to actively participate in sport.

The East End was a working-class area so there was hardly any interest in rugby. Only a few minor public schools in nearby Essex offered the sport of choice of the leisured classes. Other sports, like boxing, hockey and cycling, were popular in East London, but football quickly became king. West Ham United benefitted from this rise in the popularity of football as local people were as keen to watch as they were to play.

An interesting development in the early days was the emergence of outstanding young players like Sid Puddefoot, who had a distinguished career with the club and went on to play for England. These youngsters quickly became local heroes. The club gained a reputation for developing neighbourhood children into international stars through its academy system. In modern times Bobby Moore, Martin Peters and Trevor Brooking are the most famous, but others have included Joe Cole, Rio Ferdinand, Frank Lampard Jnr and currently Mark Noble, Freddie Sears and Jack Collison.

A six-fold increase in the population of the East End in the late 19th and early 20th centuries ensured the continued supply of promising young footballers, most of whom were West Ham fans. The growth in population of mostly working-class people also meant that attendances at Upton Park continued to rise as the club began to attract crowds of 20,000-30,000 people. The inseparable bond between the club and the community West Ham is known for had its origins in the 1920s.

This was the context for the successful season of 1922–23. If the Cup Final was the stand-out game, two Second Division matches that season were particularly memorable – and both were against local rivals Layton Orient. The two games celebrated some of West Ham's early pioneers in the history of this great club.

West Ham supporters have always seen Leyton Orient FC as a younger brother. When their own team are playing away, many Hammers fans make the short journey across Wanstead Flats to watch the O's home games. When Orient reached the semi-final of the FA Cup in 1977, there were thousands of claret-and-blue clad Orient fans at Stamford Bridge looking out for their little brother as the O's took on Arsenal.

Leyton Orient FC has an interesting East London history. The club is the second-oldest in London, after Fulham, and joined the Football League in 1905. Originally a cricket club, the O's were formed in 1888 under the name Orient, which was later changed to Clapton Orient. Club historians claim that the club name derives from the ship Britannia Orient, on which one the early committee men served. The club adopted the prefix Leyton in 1937 when it moved to its current home in Brisbane Road. The club's most successful season was 1962–63, their first and only year in the top division.

Clapton Orient played a notable part in West Ham's promotion season of 1922–23. In those days the O's home ground was the famous Spotted Dog in Clapton. The old ground was well-known to amateur footballers in the area as most of the local cup finals were played at the old pub ground. The two Second Division matches between the clubs that season defined the Hammers' year, even if they did leave the O's entrenched in the bottom six. The Hammers won the first match at Upton Park 1–0 and the return by a more comfortable 2–0, and in the process they collected a valuable four points in their bid for promotion. All three goals in the games were scored by the club's legendary centre-forward, Vic Watson.

West Ham paid Wellingborough FC the princely sum of £50 for Watson, initially as cover for fans' favourite Syd Puddefoot. Watson was born in Cambridgeshire and appeared in 505 matches for West Ham between 1920 and 1936, and he played a huge part in the club's progress in those years. But these bare facts scarcely do Watson justice – what a player he was. An old-fashioned, bustling centre-forward, he scored an incredible 326 goals in his time at the club – 74 more than his nearest rival, the great Sir Geoff Hurst.

Vic Watson's goalscoring feats are the stuff of legend at Upton Park. He holds the record for the most goals scored in a single match – six in an 8–2 victory over Leeds in 1929, which was equalled later by World Cup hero Hurst in 1968. Watson saved his best for season 1929–30, when he scored an astonishing 50 goals in just 44 appearances and achieved a personal ambition of ending the season as top scorer in Division One. His goals that year helped the Hammers to finish seventh in the top flight and reach the quarter-finals of the FA Cup.

Like many players of his era, Sgt Watson was a veteran of World War One, as were many of his Orient opponents in 1922–23. The O's lost three of their first-team players in the Somme, and many more returned with serious battlefield injuries. Hammers' club historian Brian Belton claimed that Watson was perhaps the finest centre-forward in West Ham's history. This is praise indeed when you look at the records of Geoff Hurst, Johnny Byrne and Johnny Dick. Perhaps the old soldier realised how lucky he was to be playing football after the war, and he certainly made the most of his abilities.

The West Ham side of 1922–23 was one of the best in the club's history, with players like Jimmy Ruffell, George Kay and Billy Moore supporting goalscorer in chief, Watson. Ruffell said, 'West Ham were a very good passing team. Most of the time you had an idea where the other players were – we were one of the few clubs to really practice that. Then with Watson...West Ham always had a chance at getting a goal.' Tony Hogg reminds us that Watson's goals 'were responsible for the Hammers' promotion to the First Division...and the club's appearance in the Cup Final.'

Watson scored four times in his five appearances for England. It is hard to believe, with his record, that he did not play for his country more often, except when we remember that he played in the same era as Dixie Dean and Ted Drake. West Ham fans loved Watson. He fitted perfectly into the club's attractive, fast-flowing playing, much like Hurst did many years later. Watson's goals against the Orient that season personified that way he played – the fans just knew he would score. The Stratford Express paid loyal tribute to the great number nine: 'Watson's chief worth...is in the clever way he distributes the ball. A speedy and intelligent player, he is quick to sense an opening.' It could be a description of Hurst himself, if we delete the word speedy.

Watson continued to score heavily for West Ham right through the 1920s, and in his best-ever season of 1928–29 he scored hat-tricks against Aston Villa (home and away) and Leeds United in the FA Cup, when he notched all four of his side's goals in a particularly impressive victory. He retired from the game in the mid-1930s to run a small farm in the Cambridgeshire countryside. He died aged 91 in Girton on 3 August 1988.

If Vic Watson grabbed the headlines in the two matches against the Orient, the performances of two of his clubmates are worthy of a special mention. Jimmy Ruffell was born in Yorkshire, but his family moved to East London when he was a young boy. From then on, we can safely refer to Ruffell as an East Ender. He played for Essex Road School before turning out for a number of local clubs, including Manor Park Albion and Chadwell Heath United, before signing for West Ham from the Ilford Electricity Board in 1920.

An old-fashioned outside-left, Ruffell made his West Ham debut in September 1921 in a 3–0 home victory against Port Vale. At just 5ft 9in tall, he was a classic winger, lightening fast and with great dribbling skills. He had a tremendous ability to hit pinpoint crosses to Vic Watson and the other forwards. In many respects he epitomised the club's purist commitment. With his centre-parting and mazy runs, it is impossible to overstate the contribution Ruffell made to the team through the 1920s and 1930s. He blossomed under manager Syd King and the creative influence of the man who laid the foundation stones for West Ham's philosophy of football, inspirational coach Charlie Paynter. Tony Hogg described little Jimmy as the finest winger ever to don the claret and blue. His record of appearances and goals bear no comparison.

West Ham has had some wonderful wingers in recent times – Johnny Sissons, Harry Redknapp, Stuart Slater and Johnny Ayres – but they all stand in the shadow of the great Jimmy Ruffell. He made 548 appearances from 1921–37, netted an impressive 166 League and Cup goals and regularly ended the season as the club's top scorer. His record of appearances lasted 36 years until none other than Bobby Moore surpassed it in 1973.

Given his goalscoring exploits, you would think Ruffell would have earned a hatful of England caps. In fact, he played just six times for his country, making his international debut against Scotland in 1926. Like Vic Watson, Ruffell faced tremendous competition for the England left-wing position, with the likes of Cliff Bastin and Eric Houghton keeping him out of the side. Perhaps it was playing for an unfashionable club that restricted his England appearances.

Ruffell played in the White Horse Final and was a regular in the side throughout the 1922–23 promotion season. His match-winning performance in the 6–0 drubbing of Leicester City that year gave the Hammers the goal average that eventually won them promotion. Vic Watson would probably not have scored his three goals in the Orient matches had Ruffell not laid on cross after telling cross in his usual manner.

Ruffell will be remembered at West Ham as one of their greatest-ever players. Jack Hellier, the Hammers' historian, knew Jimmy personally, and when he heard the news of Jimmy's death on 6 September 1989 at the age of 89, Hellier commented, 'As well as being one of the greats, he was also one of the nicest people you could wish to meet. The finest winger ever to play for West Ham United – a legend.

No discussion of the 1922–23 promotion year and the two wins against the Orient could fail to mention the legendary George Kay. Born in Manchester in 1891, Kay joined the Hammers in 1919 after spells with Bolton and the Belfast club Distillery. A World War One veteran, Sgt Kay served on the Western Front before being sent home suffering from shellshock. He made 237 appearances for West Ham in his seven seasons with the club, and as skipper he led his side to Wembley and promotion in 1923.

Kay was the first West Ham player to make over 200 appearances and was, arguably, the best player in the club never to play for England. He is an interesting choice as one of the best Hammers veterans because he was a northern lad, but Kay easily won the cockney hearts of the club's supporters. Kay also illustrates the way in which professional footballers of the time were beginning to move freely around the country. West Ham were now a long way from the old Thames Ironworks days and becoming a fully professional outfit.

Brian Belton acknowledged Kay's value to the club when he wrote, 'He was recognised as a deep, thoughtful man, very serious about his football...He ate, drank, slept and lived for football. His passionate attitude to the game was echoed down the years at Upton Park with Malcolm Allison, Noel Cantwell, Ron Greenwood and John Lyall – all deep thinkers about the game.'

After leading West Ham for seven successful years, Kay returned to the North with Stockport County before retiring in 1927 following a series of injuries. In 1929 he entered football management, where he enjoyed even more success than he achieved at Upton Park. After years at Luton and Southampton, Kay joined Liverpool in 1936 and stayed until 1951. He was born to club management and had tremendous success, including winning the Championship for the Reds in season 1946–47.

As Liverpool manager, Kay signed Stan Cullis, Bill Shankly and his best-ever signing, Billy Liddell. At Anfield Kay has been dubbed as the Shankly of his day and was described by Bob Paisley as one of the all-time great managers. Even Sir Matt Busby said that Kay was a huge influence on his management style. Praise does not come any higher. There is no question that Kay turned a struggling club into a Championship-winning team and laid the foundations for its later success.

George Kay died on 18 April 1954 at just 62 years old. He suffered from ill health later in life, was a chain smoker and felt the pressures and stress of football management deeply. He was a wonderful centre-half and captain at Upton Park, and he remains a true Hammers legend.

Watson, Ruffell and Kay were the heart and soul of the 1922–33 West Ham side. In the Cup Final that year, they struggled to impose their passing game on the match. Their free-flowing style was nullified by the state of the Wembley pitch, ruined by the hoofs of galloping police horses. Ruffell, the potential match-winner, was forced into the packed midfield as the numerous crowd invasions narrowed the playing area and denied the winger space to work.

The Hammers eventually gained promotion from Division Two in second place on goal average, despite losing their final game of the season at home to eventual the champions, Notts County. There were many memorable matches in 1922–23. For example, the 6–0 victory over Leicester City did wonders for the Hammers' 'goals for' column. But the two wins over the Orient, their East London neighbours, has a nice symmetry for football romantics – and they certainly boosted the promotion effort just at the right time.

**Final score:**

West Ham United: Hufton, Henderson, Young, Bishop, Kay, Tresarden, Richards, Brown, Watson, Moore, Ruffell.

# 4.

# WEST HAM UNITED

# V BLACKBURN ROVERS

## THE FA WAR CUP FINAL                8 JUNE 1940

Football matches are memorable for diverse reasons. For West Ham United, a regulation FA Cup win against Preston in 1964, European glory the following year and an outstanding performance against Arsenal in 1980 are wonderful memories. A glorious defeat, such as the match against Liverpool in Cardiff in 2006, lingers in the memory like a win rather than a loss. The 1923 White Horse Final is memorable for all the wrong reasons. The same can be said of the Hammers' victory in the Football League War Cup Final in 1940.

As a result of the outbreak of World War Two in 1939, the FA Cup was cancelled, as it had been during the Great War. Other government measures, including a ban on the gathering of crowds, brought the Football League competition to an end. Travelling any appreciable distances became tricky, while many young professional footballers signed up for active service.

The professional game had grown in popularity before the war, and many observers thought football would help with morale and every effort should be made to keep the game going. A police chief in East London remarked at the time that local football should also be encouraged. After all, he continued, no one had suggested that people should stop going to church. Police cells would be full of young men with no outlet for their energies if things like football were outlawed, he rather ruefully commented.

The authorities accepted this argument, and despite many of the grounds being taken over by the military, they gave permission for clubs to play friendly matches. Attendances were limited to 15,000, and there was a 50-mile travel limit. As there was little or no bombing in the first year of the war, the Football League decided to re-introduce a League competition. Clubs were divided into seven regional areas.

EMPIRE STADIUM

# WEMBLEY

## THE FOOTBALL LEAGUE

WAR

## CUP FINAL

BLACKBURN ROVERS

V

WEST HAM UNITED

SATURDAY, JUNE 8TH, 1940

OFFICIAL PROGRAMME • SIXPENCE

*The Official Cup Final programme cover.*

Gaining in confidence, the Football League introduced a Cup competition, and in 1940 the grimly named Football League War Cup was born. From late 1940 the football-mad public had League and Cup games to ease the pain of wartime, but complicated travel arrangements and the loss of some professional grounds to the military all made life very difficult for professional clubs.

To ease the difficulties, ground-sharing became widespread in the early part of the war. Arsenal played their home matches at White Hart Lane, the ground of their deadly London rivals, while Millwall fans were forced to make the short trip across the river to Upton Park when The Den was badly damaged by the Luftwaffe in 1940.

During the war, Upton Park was occupied by the military for long periods. The old Boleyn ground was hit during the early days of the conflict, and the West Stand, housing the club's administrative staff, suffered extensive damage. Temporary office accommodation was found in the Green Street House pub, known by all Hammers fans as the Boleyn Castle. The Boleyn was also bombed a number of times in the Blitz, which severely disrupted their programme.

In 1938 the West Ham chairman, W.J. Cearn, suggested to his first-team players that they should assist with the war effort. He encouraged them to join the local Territorials and the reserve police. If the players had accepted his suggestion, it would mean the Hammers could put out a decent first-team for the rest of the war. But to their great credit, players saw things differently. They regarded Cearn's suggestion as unpatriotic, and many of them later joined the Essex Regiment, where they were more likely to be called up for active service. Nearly 800 professional footballers were either called up or volunteered to fight, seriously depleting clubs' playing resources.

In spite of the obvious difficulties in running a club in wartime, West Ham did field a decent side, and in 1940 they managed to reach the Final of the inaugural Football League War Cup. Their Wembley opponents were Blackburn Rovers, and although crowds should have been limited to 15,000, over 43,000 fans turned up to see the big match. The vast majority of the crowd were Hammers supporters anxious to see their team on one of their rare appearances in a Cup Final.

In 1940 the national stadium was heavily involved in the war effort. Between matches, the ground was used as a temporary home to hundreds of French and Belgian war refugees. Wembley was also badly damaged when a flying bomb hit the greyhound track, releasing dozens of racing dogs into the streets of North London.

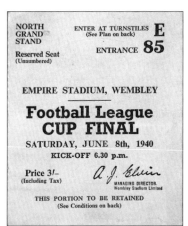

*Cup Final ticket.*

Despite all the problems, the first War Cup Final went ahead in early June. On their way to the Twin Towers, the Hammers had good wins against Chelsea, Leicester City, Huddersfield Town, Birmingham City and Fulham. The club's fanatical followers fully expected skipper Charlie Bicknell to bring the trophy back to East London. Blackburn Rovers, an old and proud club, were bound to provide stiff resistance.

The northerners had enjoyed mixed fortunes in the 1930s but returned to the top flight after

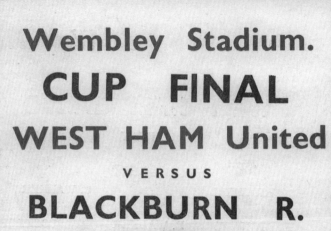

# Wembley Stadium.
## CUP FINAL
### WEST HAM United
VERSUS
## BLACKBURN R.

Kick-Off 6.30 p.m.
Saturday, June, 8th, 1940.

Souvenir

## PROGRAMME

*An un-official 'pirate' programme from the Final.*

*Action in the West Ham goalmouth during the 1940 Wartime Cup Final at Wembley against Blackburn Rovers.*

finishing champions of the old Second Division in 1938–39. They played just three League games in Division One before war was declared and play suspended.

The stage was set as the two teams were presented to Mr Alexander, 1st Lord of the Admiralty. The sides were evenly matched for most of the first half before the Hammers scored what turned out to be the decisive goal in the 34th minute. Good link-up play by new signing Len Goulden and Stan Foxall let in George Foreman for a shot on goal, which the Rovers 'keeper failed to hold. Sam Small, an ambulance manufacturer by trade, was the first to react, slipping the ball into the net beyond the helpless Barron in the Rovers' goal.

The Londoners continued to dominate after the interval, with West Ham legend Ted Fenton prominent. But, led stoutly by Bob Pryde, the Blackburn defence managed to withstand the constant threat of the Hammers' forwards, especially tricky winger Archie Macaulay. The second half brought some encouragement to Rovers supporters, who had bravely made the hazardous trip to London, as a series of goalmouth scrambles threatened an equalizer, but the breakthrough never came.

As referee Dutton blew the final whistle, West Ham became the first club to win the Football League War Cup, and they brought some much-needed cheer to the hearts of beleaguered cockneys throughout the East End.

The happy Hammers' supporters could not have imagined on that victorious day at Wembley the horrors that were to engulf them in the next 18 months.

The phoney war of the first months of the conflict was soon over, and in 1941 the East End endured seven months of the most dreadful heavy bombing. The Blitz was largely over by May 1941, but it took a heavy toll, with thousands of East Enders dead. 16,000 houses were destroyed and a quarter of all families lost their homes. The effect of the war on local communities, schools, hospitals and employment was incalculable. In 1939 the population of West Ham had been 294,278. In 1951 it was only 170,993.

Professional football did its bit during the war. Clubs like West Ham raised large amounts of money, and the game continued to be played and watched in London, despite the constant threat of German bombs. The Football League War Cup continued until the FA Cup was re-established in 1946. The 1942 Final was played at the height of the Blitz, and 60,000 plucky Londoners turned out to watch the match between Preston and Arsenal end in a draw. In the replay Preston edged out the London side 2–1 to claim the trophy.

Tom Finney, Bill Shankly, Tommy Lawton and Stanley Matthews all interrupted their professional football careers to fight for their country. Harry Goslin, an England defender, died in Italy in 1943, and the Arsenal goalkeeper lost his life in 1942 on service with the Royal Navy. The great Gunners side built by Herbert Chapman in the 1930s, which included Ted Drake and Alex James, broke up during the war. Eight Arsenal players lost their lives. Wilf Mannion, having lost half his company in Sicily, was so affected by the experience that he could hardly play football again.

At the local level football continued to be played in public parks throughout the East End and neighbouring Epping Forest. However, many of these neighbourhood grounds were dug up for planting much-needed fruit and vegetables. A few miles from Upton Park, Wanstead Flats was used as a Prisoner of War camp, and there are stories of ground staff digging up motorcycles and other wartime debris when the grass was eventually reinstated in the early 1950s.

West Ham supporters were grateful for their team's victory in 1940, but for once the result of a football match didn't seem to matter that much. At least it provided a welcome distraction from the harsh realities of wartime London.

**Final score: West Ham United 1 Blackburn Rovers 0**
West Ham United: Conway, Bicknell, C. Walker, E. Fenton, R. Walker, Cockcroft, Small, Macauley, Foreman, Goulden, Foxall.

# 5.

# WEST HAM UNITED

# V MIDDLESBOROUGH

## DIVISION TWO                    26 APRIL 1958

The Second Division is not the place where Hammers fans would normally want to go to find memorable matches, but the final match of the 1957–58 season, at Middlesborough, must be ranked as one of the most important victories by any West Ham side. The 3–2 victory over one of their closest promotion rivals saw the club back, at last, in the top flight.

'This is indeed a wonderful moment for us,' confessed proud chairman Reg Pratt. 'It is said that if you want something badly enough, you'll get it in the end. We have waited for this occasion for a very long time and now regard our present success not so much as an end but as a new beginning, a challenge, a spur to greater rewards.'

The chairman's words proved prophetic. The club were about to embark on a 19-season run in the First Division, which included the golden years of the mid-60s and the glory of Moore, Hurst and Peters. Mr Pratt could not have imagined that West Ham players would effectively win the World Cup in 1966 and play such a central part in England's finest sporting hour.

No discussion of professional football in 1958 can fail to mention the two events that, in very different ways, defined the year. That season Manchester United entered the European Cup for the first time in their history. Their talented young team enjoyed a smooth path to the quarter-finals, where they came up against Red Star Belgrade. Both legs were hard-fought and exciting matches, and despite a last-gasp penalty by the Yugoslavians, the Manchester side held on to reach the semi-finals. The plane journey home necessitated a fuel stop in Munich, where heavy snow had been falling for some time. Despite the appalling weather, the plane took off but almost immediately crashed, killing eight of the club's finest young players, including the incomparable Duncan Edwards.

With a patched-up young team, United lost the semi-final tie to Milan after bravely winning the first leg. A few weeks later the Italian club failed to prevent Real Madrid winning their third European Cup in succession. Later that season, showing enormous courage, Manchester United reached the FA Cup Final, losing 2–0 to Bolton Wanderers. The whole of the football world was shaken and saddened by the events in Munich, but the show, as they say, had to go on.

The second event was the 1958 World Cup. It was held in Sweden, and Brazil beat the host nation 5–2 in the Final – their first victory in the competition. The World Cup marked the debut on the world stage of the greatest player in the history of the game, Pele, whose career was to be so entwined with that of West Ham's greatest player, Bobby Moore. That season Moore was beginning to make his mark at Upton Park, signing professional forms for the club at the age of 17.

Pele was a precocious and unknown 17-year old in 1958, and he did not play until Brazil's final group game. The Final itself was a World Cup classic, with the match belonging to the teenage Pele, who scored two of Brazil's goals. The 1958 Final was particularly appealing because it was the first to be televised across the world. Many people who had acquired tiny black-and-white screens retain vivid memories of Pele scoring his brilliant first goal.

If the tragedy of Munich and Brazil's World Cup win defined the world of football in 1958, for West Ham fans the year brought mixed feelings of relief, hope and joy. By the end of the season they were back where they belonged, in the First Division. Their supporters could begin to lick their lips in anticipation of matches against the likes of Manchester United and Liverpool.

The story of the 1957–58 season is filled with larger-than-life characters and Hammers legends. Ted Fenton was the manager at between 1950–61. Fenton joined the club as a schoolboy with a reputation as a talented young player with an excellent goalscoring record. He represented England at schoolboy level and in 1932 made his West Ham debut at the age of 18. He played for the club up to the outbreak of war, but his career was cut short when he enlisted in the army, serving in both Burma and North Africa.

After a distinguished, if shortened, playing career, Fenton went into club management and joined Colchester in 1946 as player-manager. He returned to his beloved Upton Park in 1948 to become assistant to the legendary Charlie Paynter. It was Fenton who set the tone for the future of the club when he established the famous West Ham academy. Encouraged by Fenton, and later Ron Greenwood, the original members of the academy, Noel Cantwell, Dave Sexton, Jimmy Andrews, Malcolm Allison and Frank O'Farrell, regularly attended Casserati's café close to the Boleyn ground, where they would talk for hours about technique, tactics and training methods. The result of these lively discussions was the club success of the mid-1960s. None of this would have happened without Fenton's penetrating football brain.

Unusual for managers of his day, Fenton took coaching seriously and encouraged players to take FA coaching badges to improve their awareness of the game. Seven

*A step up for West Ham. The first-team squad on the eve of the 1958-59 season. From top to bottom they are: Ernie Gregory, John Bond, Malcolm Pyke, Andy Nelson, Vic Keeble, Noel Cantwell, John Dick, Ken Brown, Bill Lansdowne, Andy Malcolm, Mike Grice, Malcolm Musgrove, John Smith, Bill Dare.*

members of the FA Cup-winning team of 1964 had either been signed by Fenton or came through the Academy, but his greatest triumph as a manager has to be gaining promotion to the First Division in 1958.

Like political lives, most managerial careers end in failure, and Fenton's was no exception. He left West Ham in March 1961 in mysterious circumstances, which have never been properly explained to this day. The team's form had been poor and

*Ted Fenton chats to players of newly-promoted West Ham as they arrive at Upton Park for the first day of training in July 1958.*

the manager's health had suffered, and after 11 years at the club he was eventually replaced by Ron Greenwood. Fenton left Upton Park for Southend United, where he stayed for four undistinguished years before he was sacked in 1965. Ted Fenton died in a car accident in 1992 at Loughborough, on his way to a family reunion.

Fenton's place in the history of West Ham United FC is secure, and his contribution to the club's success in the 1960s and their famous playing style cannot be exaggerated. But football is really about footballers rather than managers, and the club owes a huge debt to the players of that era. Three in particular stand out for special mention, and all three played in the historic win against Middlesborough in 1958.

Malcolm 'Muzzie' Musgrove was one of the last generation of professional footballers to be called up for National Service, a fate that escaped Bobby Moore, born a few years later. Musgrove was a vital member of the Second Division Championship team of 1958 and enjoyed 10 very successful seasons at the club. An outside-left by trade, Malcolm would often switch inside to stiffen the midfield. He made his debut in 1954 against Brentford and soon established himself in the side, gaining a reputation as a prolific goalscorer.

Muzzie was extremely popular at Upton Park and went on to make 301 League and Cup appearances for the Hammers, scoring an impressive 89 goals. Only the incomparable Jimmy Ruffels (164) scored more goals from the wing. His game flourished playing alongside the likes of Vic Keeble, Malcolm Allison, John Bond, Ken Brown and Frank O'Farrell, and his skilful play was integral to the Hammers' classic academy football.

Like many West Ham players coming to the end of the playing careers, Musgrove left in 1962 for Leyton Orient and later became a coach at Brisbane Road. He became well-respected in the game and that same year was appointed chairman of the PFA. After leaving Orient in 1968, Musgrove went on to coach at Aston Villa and Leicester City, where he became assistant manager to former teammate O'Farrell.

Farrell moved to Manchester United in 1971 and took his old friend with him, but Musgrove was desperate to run his own team and left a year later for the manager's job at Torquay United. From Torquay he spent some time in the US before returning to train as a physiotherapist, practising at several clubs before joining Plymouth Argyle as coach. In the mid-1970s he finally left the game to live in retirement in South Devon. Musgrove suffered from Alzheimer's disease and died in a Paignton nursing home on 14 September 2007, aged 74. West Ham United had lost one their all-time greats.

During Fenton's army days, he discovered Johnny Dick. The Scot was born in Glasgow's tough Govan district, the same neighbourhood as Alex Ferguson. He was signed by the Hammers at the end of his National Service and played for the club between 1953 and 1962. Dick crossed the generations, and late in his career he played with some of the next generation of Hammers stars, including Bobby Moore, Martin Peters, Geoff Hurst, Johnny Byrne, John Bond and Kenny Brown. He became the club's joint-third highest goalscorer, playing 351 games with a remarkable 166 goals.

Dick was made captain of the club by Ted Fenton and became the first West Ham player to be picked for Scotland to play against England, replacing the injured Dennis Law. The England team in that match included Bobby Charlton and Billy Wright, gaining his 100th cap. Unfortunately, Dick had few opportunities in the match, which England won 1-0.

Always a popular local figure, Dick married his young wife Sue in Barking Abbey Church in 1956, and they set up home in Hainault with their two daughters, Jennifer and Gillian. Before it became popular, Dick became interested in the country life found out in Essex, and he developed a passion for animals and wildlife in general.

In 1962, towards the end of his career, Dick moved to Brentford for a fee of £17,500. He played for the West London club for three seasons before taking up a sports development job for the old Inner London Education Authority in Hackney.

Dick took early retirement in 1992 due to ill health. Doctors recommended a strict walking schedule for his heart problem, and he was often seen walking round the lake and golf course in Hainault Forest. Dick died in 2000, and the family had a seat dedicated to his memory by Hainault Lake. His ashes were scattered close to the seat, and a memorial oak tree planted to provide shade for visitors. John Dick was an adopted East London and Essex man, and he was a hugely respected figure in the area. He remains a West Ham legend, and it was his goal in the final match of the 1957–58 season to take his club back to the First Division.

What a contribution Vic 'The Camel' Keeble made to the Hammers' 1957–58 promotion-winning season. The Colchester-born centre-forward was not the most skilful or graceful of number nines, but there was no better header of the ball in the Football League. One journalist at the time jokingly wrote that Keeble 'would even take a penalty with his head if he had the choice'.

Keeble's goalscoring exploits at Colchester came to the attention of many of the top clubs. Newcastle United had been following Keeble's progress for some time, and they snapped him up for a bargain price £15,000 at the end of the 1951–52 season. Keeble was an immediate success at Newcastle. He played in the 1953 Cup Final against Manchester City, where his teammates included such great football names as Jimmy Scoular and Jackie Milburn. In 1954–55 Keeble hit top form and finished the season as leading scorer for the Geordies, with 29 goals in just 36 games.

Keeble later recalled, 'My partnership with Jackie (Milburn) was great. I'd nod them on and he could really move...and had two terrific feet...the ball would go in like a rocket. Milburn repaid the compliment, he scored so many goals with his nut that I swear he had studs in his forehead.'

The following season Keeble was troubled by injuries and scored just four goals. His confidence suffered, not helped by the fickle Geordie fans, who cruelly nicknamed him 'Feeble Keeble', although it was true that his ball-skills were at best limited and at worst laughable.

Meanwhile, Keeble's old manager at Colchester, Ted Fenton, now at West Ham, became aware of Keeble's problems at Newcastle, and he stepped in and snapped up his old centre-forward for the bargain price of £10,000. Keeble arrived at the East London club mid-season, at which point the Hammers had a miserable nine points from 11 games. Following Keeble's introduction into the side, they lost only three of their next 31 games.

The Camel formed a great partnership with Johnny Dick, and the pair scored 40 goals between them in the 1957–58 season. Keeble transformed Fenton's side, scoring 23 goals, and his improved all-round play sent the Hammers into the First Division. A teammate said at the time, 'When Vic Keeble came he turned us around – it was his goals that got us up.'

Keeble's rich vein of goalscoring form continued when he scored the Hammers' first goal in the First Division for over a quarter of a century. His goal against Portsmouth in the opening game of the new season sent the 40,000 Upton Park crowd into raptures of delight. With the Keeble/Dick partnership continuing to flourish, the Hammers ended the 1958–59 season in sixth place.

Sadly, Keeble injured his back in October 1959 and played one only more game for the club before retiring in January 1960. He began and finished his playing days with Ted Fenton and loved his time at Upton Park. He later spoke about giving a youthful Geoff Hurst a lift to training, and of working with Malcolm Allison and the young Bobby Moore.

Aged just 29, Keeble flirted with football reporting before joining up with his old club, Colchester, as general manager. He later moved to Chelmsford City in a similar position before finally retiring in 1994. Fenton should have the last word on Vic Keeble's importance as a vintage Hammer: 'I didn't seriously think of promotion until after I signed Vic Keeble, then I thought it would be possible.'

The West Ham side that Saturday at Middlesborough included Dick, Musgrove, and Keeble, together with such club legends as Ken Brown and Noel Cantwell. The Hammers started strongly, and Dick gave his team an early lead with a deft back-heel for his 21st goal of the season. Musgrove, probing from left midfield and controlling the game as he often did, added a second. Not to be left out, Keeble sealed the victory and promotion late in the game. The champions headed home with an impressive 23 wins and 11 draws out of their 42 games. The Hammers thoroughly deserved their success, having scored a striking 101 goals during the season.

Over 1,000 Hammers fans crowded onto the platform at King's Cross Station to welcome their conquering heroes back from Middlesborough. They had real reason to rejoice, having been rooted in the Second Division since 1932. Under Ted Fenton, and then Ron Greenwood, the club went from strength to strength, with their unique playing style winning fans across the world. Promotion ushered in a new glorious era for the Hammers. From 1964–66 iconic captain Bobby Moore lifted the FA Cup and the European Cup-Winners' Cup for West Ham and the World Cup for England.

**Final score: West Ham United 3 Middlesborough 0**
West Ham United: Gregory, Bond, Cantwell, Malcolm, Allison (captain), O'Farrell, Hooper, Dare, Dick, Foan, Tucker.

# 6.

# WEST HAM UNITED

# V LIVERPOOL / V COVENTRY CITY
## FA YOUTH CUP                    1963 / 1999

The FA Youth Cup was set up by the FA in 1953 as a national competition for young players under the age of 18. The competition is now dominated by teams from the Premier League academies, but over 400 clubs compete for the coveted trophy each season. Manchester United won the inaugural contest and have won it a record nine times since.

The tournament has been a springboard into the highest level of the game for many top British players, including George Best, John Barnes, Ryan Giggs, David Beckham, Frank Lampard Jnr, Michael Owen, Steven Gerrard, Joe Cole and Wayne Rooney. The Manchester United team that won the competition in 1991–92 famously became the all-conquering Alex Ferguson side of the 1990s.

West Ham's Under-18 team have reached the final on seven occasions, beating Liverpool in 1963, Tottenham in 1981, and Coventry in 1999. The final is played over two legs and attracts crowds of over 20,000. A book of the most memorable matches of West Ham United would be incomplete without highlighting the achievements of the Hammers' youth system. Known as the original Academy, the club's youth policy has become a model for developing local young talent. In past years the best Hammers sides have contained a majority of local lads who could either walk to Upton Park from home or, at worst, hop on a bus. Bobby Moore, Martin Peters, John Charles, Trevor Brooking, Harry Redknapp, Frank Lampard Snr, Ronnie Boyce and Mark Noble are just a few of the youngsters who were born within a few miles of the Boleyn.

In more recent years the club has tended to recruit young players and trade them off for a fat profit. Lampard Jnr, Ferdinand, Carrick and Joe Cole all played in the FA Youth Cup for the Hammers and all were sold to the highest bidder, but back in the 1960s the likes of Moore, Brooking and Hurst were nurtured as the future of the club.

The West Ham much-admired youth policy was started by Ted Fenton in the late 1950s and further developed by Ron Greenwood, John Lyall and Harry Redknapp, but arguably the most influential coach at Upton Park, and the man most responsible for the purist reputation of the club, was Malcolm Allison. The young coach led Tuesday and Thursday evening training sessions in the forecourt outside the Boleyn ground, which inspired the Hammers youngsters. Allison, a great admirer of the 1950s Hungarian side, was a forward-thinking coach. He introduced lightweight boots, smaller shorts and lighter shirts before any other English club. More than anyone, Allison helped nurture the great talent of Bobby Moore and dozens of other young players at the club.

Fenton, Allison and Greenwood were rewarded in the 1960s, when the club reached three consecutive cup finals. Tony Carr has picked up the baton in more recent years and has led a renaissance of youth development at the club. In 2010 Carr was awarded a well-deserved OBE in recognition of his work with young players.

At the centre of the Academy in the 1960s and 1970s was the legendary chief scout, Wally St Pier. St Pier joined the club as a centre-half in 1929 and became its chief scout in 1948. He was born in nearby Ilford and took pride in having an encyclopaedic knowledge of junior football in the area.

As Brian Belton points out in his book, Men of '64, St Pier stood on countless windy and wet touchlines of school pitches on Wanstead Flats, Hackney Marshes and West Ham Park, unearthing such jewels as Moore, Hurst, Brooking and Peters. West Ham and England owe St Pier and his scouting predecessor, Reg Bevin, a huge debt. Three of his discoveries played in the 1966 World Cup-winning side, scoring all four goals between them. The 1964 Hammers side was made up of local lads, claret-and-blue through and through, and was the last to field 11 Englishman in every round of the FA Cup. Was this a good thing? If we look at the plight of the current England side, perhaps it was.

### 1963 FA Youth Cup Final

West Ham United v Liverpool

The first leg of the 1963 Final was played at Anfield, and the young Hammers were clearly intimidated by the atmosphere created by the hostile home fans in The Kop. They went behind in the first few minutes. The soft southerners reputation was confirmed for the Scousers when their side scored a second in the 35th minute. The few Irons fans in the crowd must have feared the worst as their highly rated youngsters looked to be heading for a hiding.

Just when the Reds threatened to overwhelm them, Billy Droyden pulled one back for the Hammers. The claret-and-blue boys began to rediscover their passing game and slowly crept back into the match. At the beginning of the second half, soon-to-be Liverpool legend Tommy Smith set the tone for his career at Anfield. His tackle on Johnny Sissons reduced the potential Hammers' match-winner to walking pace for the rest of the game.

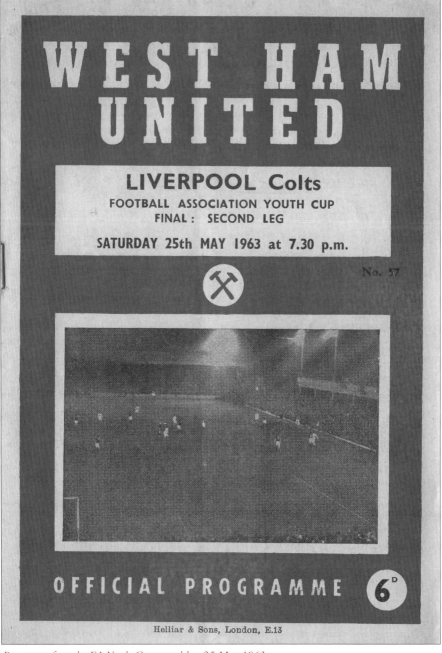

*Programme from the FA Youth Cup second leg, 25 May 1963.*

Despite being driven on by the heroic defending of skipper John Charles, the young Irons began to flag. But just when their fans thought they might head for the second leg at Upton Park only a goal down, Liverpool scored a third. This would have shattered most sides, but this group of East Enders was clearly made of strong stuff. They dominated the last fifteen minutes of the match, hitting the post through Peter Bennett, while the tearaway winger Redknapp came close to pulling a goal back in the last few minutes. Being 3–1 down after the first leg was not good, but at times the youthful Hammers side showed they had the measure of their opponents. They could look forward to the Second leg with some degree of optimism.

Over 25,000 people crammed into three sides of the Boleyn crowd as the faithful Hammers fans turned out to get behind their youngsters. The boys would need all the support they could get in their uphill struggle to beat a powerful Liverpool side. The club were not expecting such a turn-out and left one side of the stadium closed – along with most of the refreshment outlets in the ground.

Spurred on by the large partisan crowd, the young Hammers began nervously but settled when Trevor Dawkins fired a shot through the crowded penalty area into the Liverpool net. The final was now wide open, and the home side surged forward urged on again by man of the tie skipper John Charles, who seemed to be everywhere. But just when the young Irons looked as though they would level the score, disaster struck. The Reds scored two breakaway goals in three minutes to give them a thumping 5–2 aggregate lead.

The quietened home crowd regained their spirits just before half-time when the big centre-forward Martin Britt headed his side back in contention. The atmosphere in the ground at the break was something special. The fans were enjoying the occasion hugely and recognised that their team was giving everything, win or lose.

The Hammers started the second half strongly, and in the 60th minute the ever-dangerous Britt scored his second to bring his side just one goal behind. In the last ten minutes, with Redknapp running riot on the wing and Charles screaming at his team to get forward, the young Irons battered their Scouse opponents. Yet another mazy run down the right by Redknapp exposed the Liverpool defence, and his superb cross was met by Britt, whose header flew into the net, completing a wonderful hat-trick for the young centre-forward.

With the game heading for extra-time or a replay – no one seemed to know – man of the match Redknapp set off on another jinking raid down the right. He coolly picked out Britt again, and the young centre-forward rammed in the cross to win the match for his team. Upton Park went mad as the crowd realised the score had finished 6–5 on aggregate in their favour. The Hammers had won the FA Youth Cup for the first time.

On an unforgettable night, Martin Britt's four goals won the match, ably assisted by Redknapp's brilliant wing play and captain Charles' courageous leadership. Ron Greenwood described the win that night as 'wonderful – the best night of my life'. He was right to be excited as 10 members of 1963 Cup-winning side went on to play for the senior team.

Britt was in the First team at the age of 18 but sadly was soon sold to Blackburn, where a serious knee injury wrecked his career. Brilliant in the air, his four-goal display at Upton Park that night ended up as the high point of his career. Perhaps he could never be the same player without the deadly crosses of Sissons and Redknapp to provide his goalscoring chances. But he certainly gave Anfield iron-man Tommy Smith a run around that night.

Less famous local youngsters also made their mark in the Youth team but in different and sometimes more interesting ways. John 'Charlo' Charles, the skipper of the 1963 Youth side, was one of nine children born in Canning Town. He made his first-team debut against Blackburn Rovers in 1963 at the age of 19 and made 142 appearances for the club during the 1960s. Interestingly, Charles played most of his games for West Ham at full-back, alongside Bobby Moore, and was a member of the all-conquering squad that triumphed in the FA Cup and European Cup-Winners' Cup.

Charles was one of the first black players to break into top-flight professional football, not that this would have troubled him in the slightest. His greatest performance for West Ham remains his captaincy of the FA Youth Cup winning side of 1963. He was released by club at the age of 26, but instead of continuing his career in football, he opted to start a greengrocer business in East London. Charles died in 2002, aged just 57, after a long and courageous battle with lung cancer. West Ham historian Brian Belton was so inspired by Charles' bravery that he wrote a moving tribute to the full-back entitled Johnny the One, one of the full-back's two nicknames. At the time of his death, the club sent their sincere condolences to John's wife, Carol, and her children, and friends and colleagues also expressed their sadness at his sad, untimely death. Brian Dear, who had known Charles for 40 years, was at Charles' bedside in Barkingside when he passed away and said, 'John was quite simply a lovely, lovely man who was West Ham through and through...the last 18 months have been very hard for him...it's terribly sad news.'

John's brother, Clive, was a full-back like his older brother, and he made 14 appearances for the Hammers between 1970–73. He never became as famous as some of his more illustrious teammates, but in many ways his story is more remarkable. Finding competition for places at Upton Park a little fierce, Clive decided to join the fledgling North American Soccer League, where he played two seasons with Montreal Olympique and met his future wife, Clarena. Frustrated by the standard of the game in the US, Charles returned to Britain in 1964 and made over 100 appearances for Cardiff City, many of them as captain.

The younger Charles had enjoyed the life in the US, even if the football remained in the development stage, so in 1978 he returned and signed for Oregon's Portland Timbers. He played out the rest of his career in America before injury forced him to retire. Clive had always enjoyed coaching, so he was delighted to be offered a job teaching football in a high school in Oregon. It was to prove a major turning point in his life.

Following three successful years as a school coach, Charles was offered the job that would transform his career and allow him to develop his coaching skills to the full. He transformed the little-known University of Portland into America's most powerful college football team. In his time at the college, Portland won both the women's and men's National Championship and produced dozens of international footballers. He coached the US Under-23 men's and women's teams, and he was assistant coach to the national men's team at the 1998 World Cup in Paris. Against all the odds, his Under-23 men's side finished fourth in the Sydney Olympics. Clive Charles became a highly respected teacher and coach, and he made a major contribution to the rise of the US as a serious football nation. His reputation in the world of football in America is legendary.

Charles's remarkable story was tragically cut short when he died of prostate cancer at his Portland home in 2003. He was just 51 years of age. As a coach, he was far more interested in developing individuals than purely winning matches, and as a result he was treasured by his players. He created a football dynasty at Portland as Tiffeny Milbrett, one of America's hottest properties at the time, testified: 'I wouldn't have gone there if not for him. I didn't go for the school, I didn't go for the education, I went because Clive asked me to. I said yes within a half-second. When you talk about guidance, support, trust and love, those things you get from your parents. I didn't have a father in my life. He filled that void.'

American international and Portland graduate Shannon MacMillan said of her mentor, 'Clive turned my life around. Through his teaching, friendship and love, he became the father-figure I never had. He's an incredible and special man. I am where I am as a person and a player because of Clive. I love him.'

Towards the end of his live Charles talked frankly about his illness and his treatment. He

*Team sheet from the FA Youth Cup second leg, 25 May 1963.*

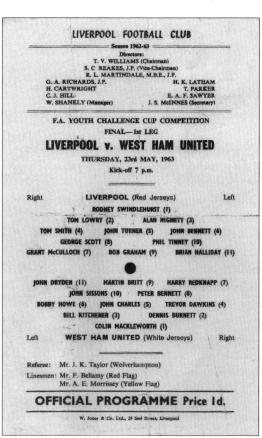

LIVERPOOL FOOTBALL CLUB

Season 1962-63

Directors:
T. V. WILLIAMS (Chairman)
S. C REAKES, J.P. (Vice-Chairman)
R. L. MARTINDALE, M.B.E., J.P.
G. A. RICHARDS, J.P.          H. K. LATHAM
H. CARTWRIGHT              T. PARKER
C. J. HILL                E. A. F. SAWYER
W. SHANKLY (Manager)      J. S. McINNES (Secretary)

F.A. YOUTH CHALLENGE CUP COMPETITION
FINAL—1st LEG

**LIVERPOOL v. WEST HAM UNITED**

THURSDAY, 23rd MAY, 1963

Kick-off 7 p.m.

Right          **LIVERPOOL** (Red Jerseys)          Left
RODNEY SWINDLEHURST (1)
TOM LOWRY (2)          ALAN HIGNETT (3)
TOM SMITH (4)    JOHN TURNER (5)    JOHN BENNETT (6)
GEORGE SCOTT (8)          PHIL TINNEY (10)
GRANT McCULLOCH (7)    BOB GRAHAM (9)    BRIAN HALLIDAY (11)

●

JOHN DRYDEN (11)    MARTIN BRITT (9)    HARRY REDKNAPP (7)
JOHN SISSONS (10)    PETER BENNETT (8)
BOBBY HOWE (6)    JOHN CHARLES (5)    TREVOR DAWKINS (4)
BILL KITCHENER (3)          DENNIS BURNETT (2)
COLIN MACKLEWORTH (1)
Left    **WEST HAM UNITED** (White Jerseys)    Right

Referee:  Mr. J. K. Taylor (Wolverhampton)
Linesmen: Mr. F. Bellamy (Red Flag)
Mr. A. E. Morrissey (Yellow Flag)

**OFFICIAL PROGRAMME Price 1d.**

W. Jones & Co. Ltd., 29 Seel Street, Liverpool

emphasised how important his family was to him, and he would have been proud that his daughter Sarah became a Portland player in the 1990s. Charles was inducted into the Oregon Sports Hall of Fame in 2003.

The Charles brothers came from a huge East End family, and they truly made their mark on the world of football. The club, supporters and the East End in general can be immensely proud of their achievements.

Final score: West Ham United 6 Liverpool 5
West Ham United: Mackleworth, Burnett, Kitchener, Dawkins, Charles, Howe, Redknapp, Bennett, Britt, Sissons, Dryden.

## 1999 FA Youth Cup Final
West Ham United v Coventry City

The young Hammers won the Youth Cup a second time in 1981, but the club's golden generation of Rio Ferdinand and Frank Lampard Jnr, of whom so much was expected, were well-beaten by a strong Liverpool side in the 1996 Final. The club reached the Final yet again in 1999. The team included Michael Carrick and the hottest prospect seen at the club since Bobby Moore, Joe Cole. It is difficult to exaggerate the excitement generated at West Ham by the emergence of the outrageously gifted forward. Some the comparisons – Pele, Maradona and Best –were a little over the top, but the anticipation was genuine as the young Cole appeared to be in a different class to anyone of his own age.

In an earlier round, against Arsenal at Highbury in front of just 600 people, Cole, who had already made his first-team debut, was the difference between the two sides, floating around in the space just behind his strikers to brilliant effect. With Cole in their side, the young Irons could look forward to the Final with real confidence.

The Final proved something of an anticlimax, lacking the

*Programme cover from the first leg of the 1999 FA Youth Cup.*

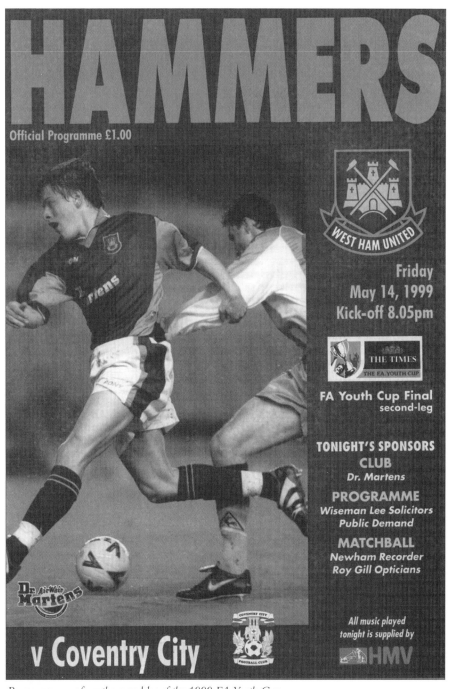

HAMMERS

Official Programme £1.00

v Coventry City

Friday
May 14, 1999
Kick-off 8.05pm

THE TIMES
THE FA YOUTH CUP

FA Youth Cup Final
second-leg

TONIGHT'S SPONSORS
CLUB
Dr. Martens

PROGRAMME
Wiseman Lee Solicitors
Public Demand

MATCHBALL
Newham Recorder
Roy Gill Opticians

All music played
tonight is supplied by

HMV

*Programme cover from the second leg of the 1999 FA Youth Cup.*

*Teamsheet from the 1999 Youth Cup Final.*

THE TIMES
THE F.A. YOUTH CUP

**Times FA Youth Cup Final 2nd Leg**
**West Ham United (3) Vs Coventry City (0)**
**TEAMSHEET**
14th May, 1999

| WEST HAM UNITED | | | COVENTRY CITY | |
|---|---|---|---|---|
| 1 | Stephen Bywater | GK | Chris Kirkland | 1 |
| 2 | Adam Newton | | Robert Betts | 2 |
| 3 | Sam Taylor | C | Thomas Codworth | 3 |
| 4 | Tyrell Forbes | | Gerrard Mooney | 4 |
| 5 | Ezomo Iriekpen | C | Callum Davenport | 5 |
| 6 | Stevland Angus | | Mark Burrows | 6 |
| 7 | Michael Ferrante | | Matthew Lewis | 7 |
| 8 | Joe Cole | | Craig Pead | 8 |
| 9 | Bertie Brayley | | Stephen McPhee | 9 |
| 10 | Richard Garcia | | Gary McSheffrey | 10 |
| 11 | Michael Carrick | | Mark Graham | 11 |

| SUBSTITUTES | | | SUBSTITUTES | |
|---|---|---|---|---|
| 13 | Lee Richards | GK | Adam Mehmet | 13 |
| 12 | Anwar Uddin | | Daire Doyle | 12 |
| 14 | Ashley Cooper | | Nathan Thompson | 14 |
| 15 | Francis Birch | | Craig Strachan | 15 |
| 16 | Steve Clarke | | Martin Grant | 16 |

Referee: Mr Rob Harris
Assistant Referees: John Holbrook, Michael Thorpe
Fourth Official: Gary Parish

MMA, 48 Gray's Inn Road, London WC1X 8LT  Tel: 0171 831 3027  Fax: 0171 831 5277

drama of 1963. The Hammers won the first leg at Highfield Road 3–0, reducing the second game at Upton Park to a formality. But what a display the youngsters produced in front of a proud home crowd. Their performance at the Boleyn that night showed that the youth coaching set-up, which had launched the careers of some of the best players in England and now Carrick and Cole, was still producing young players of the highest quality.

The 1999 generation was probably the best Youth side ever, mainly because they had Joe Cole. He ran the show at

*Happy Hammers Youth team after beating Coventry City to win the FA Youth Cup in May 1999.*

Upton Park, supported by outstanding performances from Carrick and defender Adam Newton. The Hammers opened the scoring in the second minute, when Bertie Brayley steered in Newton's cross. Not to be outdone, Newton broke forward and added a brilliant goal of his own. Then Garcia scored from the spot, and, with three further goals in the second half, the score finished 6–0 on the night and a staggering 9–0 on aggregate. The young Coventry side were simply overwhelmed by the sheer brilliance of Cole and his team. The first-team manager, Harry Redknapp, watching from the stands, could hardly conceal his delight.

The 21,000 Hammers supporters in the ground cheered their young team to the echo, anticipating the golden future that lay ahead for the club. Unfortunately the club sold their greatest prospect since Bobby Moore to Chelsea. He has never been the same player since.

**Final score: West Ham United 9 Coventry City 0**

West Ham United: Bywater, Newton, Taylor, Forbes, Irikpen, Angus, Carrick, Cole, Garcia, Brayley, Ferrate, Uddin.

# 7.

# WEST HAM UNITED

# V MANCHESTER UNITED

## FA CUP SEMI-FINAL                    14 MARCH 1964

There is a grainy old film clip of this match on Pathé News. We see the teams coming out onto the pitch and watch, intrigued, as the two captains, Denis Law and Bobby Moore, toss the coin for choice of ends. The Hammers are in their classic claret-and-blue hooped away shirts, with Manchester United in an unfamiliar all-white strip.

Law wins the toss and play starts in torrential rain as the camera pans round to bring into view unprotected terraces, including the famous Hillsborough Spion Kop, which, in those days, towered high above one end of the ground. Most of the spectators are sporting club scarves and peak caps, giving the impression that the match was during the immediate post-war period rather than at the height of the swinging '60s. The rain was hurled into the faces of the fans by the howling wind coming off the Yorkshire Moors, but despite the atrocious weather both sides did their best to play football. They knew no other way.

Matt Busby's side begin the match clear favourites, particularly as they had beaten the Hammers 2–0 at Upton Park just seven days earlier. They must have left East London thinking their appearance in another Wembley Final was done and dusted – they just had to turn up in Sheffield to claim their place. West Ham had other ideas, as skipper Bobby Moore, leading by example, as

SHEFFIELD WEDNESDAY F. C. LTD.
HILLSBOROUGH, SHEFFIELD — LEPPINGS LANE
FOOTBALL ASSOCIATION CHALLENGE CUP
SEMI-FINAL

ENTRANCE

Saturday, 14th March
KICK-OFF 3 o'clock

**B**

GROUND 5/-

Issued subject to the Rules, Regulations and
Bye-Laws of the Football Association
No Ticket exchanged nor money refunded

N? 03017

*General Manager and Secretary*
THIS PORTION TO BE RETAINED

YOU ARE REQUESTED TO TAKE
UP YOUR POSITION THIRTY
MINUTES BEFORE KICK-OFF

*Semi-final ticket.*

SATURDAY
MARCH 14th 1964
KICK-OFF 3.0 p.m.

1/-
OFFICIAL PROGRAMME

*Semi-Final*

MANCHESTER UNITED
VERSUS
WEST HAM UNITED

*at Hillsborough*

*Semi-final programme cover.*

we would expect, timed his tackles to perfection and calmly rolled his passes into the Hammers' midfield.

The Old Trafford side that day included the all-conquering trio of Charlton, Best and Law, who were to form the core of the European Cup-winning side of 1968. Despite the strength of their opponents, the Hammers supporters travelled in hope, as always, and the strains of Bubbles can just about be made out on the film clip. The Irons' line-up had a familiar look, and Ron Greenwood was able to field his strongest side. Hurst and Byrne provided the goal threat, with Brabrook and Sissons on the wings, and a midfield of the well-organised and industrious pair, Boyce and Eddie Bovington, supplemented by the often deep-lying Byrne.

Boyce and Bovington were the engine room of the side. Both players were excellent passers and were patient in their distribution. They knew how to look after the ball. Time and time again the two midfielders would pick up a short pass from Moore and move the ball out to Sissons and Brabrook. Alternatively, they would drill passes through the channels to Hurst, certain in the knowledge that the centre-forward would hold the ball up until Byrne joined him in attack.

The Hammers had enjoyed a relatively untroubled route to the semi-final, seeing off Charlton, Leyton Orient, Swindon and Burnley on their way to Hillsborough. Coping with the sublime skills of Law, Best and Charlton would be a different story for the attack-minded Londoners, but from the first few minutes they showed they were more than up to the challenge.

Denis Law had an early chance, but his header was easily held by Jim Standen. In the 19th minute George Best skipped through the stodgy pitch and rattled the crossbar with his shot – a sure sign of the danger posed by the Manchester number seven. The players trudged off at half-term in the pouring rain with the score at 0–0. The Hammers had been in defiant mood in the first half, and they grew in confidence as half-time approached. Hurst and Byrne went close on three occasions as they began to worry the Reds' rearguard and ask them a few questions. The Irons fans were buoyed by their team's first-half performance. They knew that this was a very good West Ham side.

The second half brought early problems for the Hammers when centre-forward David Herd, following a goalmouth scramble, shot just wide of the far post. But the Hammers began to control the game and dominate possession. The Manchester goal came under increasing pressure as Byrne, Bovington and Boyce began to get a firm grip on midfield, using Sissons and Brabrook out wide whenever they could.

In the 55th minute, after a spell of passing around the Reds' penalty area, the ball came to Ronnie Boyce, who looked up and hit a dipping drive just under the bar and into the net. West Ham were 1–0 up with just over 35 minutes left – could they possibly hold on against one of the best teams in Europe? For the next few minutes Charlton, Law and Best threw everything at Bobby Moore and his men as they searched desperately for the equalizer.

The Hammers soon made their opponents pay for their desperation. They gained some relief when one of their rare attacks went out for a corner. Johnny Sissons took the kick quickly out to Jack Burkett who sent a delicate chip into the path of Ronnie Boyce. As the ball reached the midfielder he headed it firmly into the net without breaking stride, and the West Ham fans went wild. Two nil ahead in the 65th minute, surely they couldn't lose now.

With the Twin Towers looming, Manchester United fought back. Chasing a lost cause, Denis Law slid into Jim Standen, causing play to be held up for five minutes. When play restarted Law took advantage of West Ham's groggy 'keeper to reduce the deficit. In the heart-stopping last 12 minutes, the Reds battered the Hammers' defence, who were in no mood to surrender their hard-fought lead.

In the midst of the nervy action, Bobby Moore stood calm and defiant. Just as he was to do in the last minutes of the World Cup Final two years later, the skipper turned defence into attack in a heartbeat. He picked up the ball from Jim Standen late in the game, moved a few yards forward and hit a defence-splitting pass into the path of the ever-alert Hurst. The centre-forward burst through the Manchester rearguard and hit a crisp, low shot past Gaskell's despairing right hand.

Moore's men had made it through to the FA Cup Final for the first time since 1923 – and how the fans celebrated as their beloved Irons for once played to their full potential when it really mattered. The 1964 West Ham side was as good as any team in Europe on their day, with Trevor Brooking and Billy Bonds still to come. A lack of consistency was their enduring problem, but on that day in Sheffield they were irresistible. It was probably the best result in the club's history to date.

The celebrations in the Boleyn Castle and other pubs across the East End went on late into that Saturday night. Meanwhile, the players were making their way back from Sheffield by train and, being West Ham players, they wanted to join in the fans' partying.

The Hammers side of the 1960s were a close-knit bunch, with just a few players, notably Peters, Sissons and Burkett, on the fringe of the action. The players drank regularly in pubs around Upton Park, spent mornings in the Casseratti café in the Barking Road or enjoyed card schools on long away trips. Moore and Byrne were at the heart of the socialising, which more often than not involved large quantities of lager.

As club captain, Moore believed that team-bonding was essential. However, manager Greenwood strongly disapproved of what he perceived to be a 'drinking culture' at the club. His displeasure was apparent on the train back to London following the victory against Manchester United. Moore noticed that Greenwood had become uncharacteristically emotional on the return journey and recalled, 'It was the only time I ever saw Ron emotional. The train was packed – a madhouse.'

Players were mingling with fans and enjoying a few celebratory beers, while Greenwood sat alone in the dining car. Moore asked his manager what was wrong and Greenwood replied, 'We've got this far without all these hangers-on. We don't need these people.' Moore argued that these people were the club's fans. They had travelled all the way to Sheffield and were among the most loyal and passionate supporters in the country – they have earned their celebrations. But Greenwood was unmoved – a further indication of the differences between the two men.

Perhaps Greenwood had a point. At the heart of his frustration with his players was the team's infuriating inconsistency. On their day they could beat anybody, as they showed in the semi-final against Manchester United. Although Greenwood would have enjoyed his team's performance at Hillsborough, he would have been acutely aware that the Hammers finished the League season in a lowly 14th position. The upright Greenwood could never understand that his players loved pubs, clubs and gambling almost as much as they loved football, and he believed that this was at the heart of their frustrating form. Others argued – that was just the West Ham way. But at that moment the Hammers were in the Cup Final and could look forward to the 1964–65 season with realistic hopes of more success.

**Final score: Manchester United 1 West Ham United 3**
West Ham United: Standen, Bond, Burkett, Bovington, Brown, Moore, Byrne, Brabrook, Boyce, Hurst, Sissons.

# 8.

# WEST HAM UNITED
# V PRESTON NORTH END

## 1964 FA CUP FINAL                    2 MAY 1964

In 1964, with the decade in full swing, the Hammers were about to embark on the most successful period in their history. The East London club even became mildly fashionable as their brand of attacking football began to catch the eye of the football public. The 1966 World Cup was still two years away, but as early as 1964 top footballers were attracting celebrity status. George Best became known as the fifth Beatle, and the young West Ham captain, Bobby Moore, was beginning to attract the interest of a wider audience.

The 1960s were an extraordinary time. The Beatles charmed America in 1964 with their first album, and by the end of that year the Liverpool musical sensation occupied all top five places in the US singles charts. Their dazzling achievements paved the way for the success of the Rolling Stones' debut album.

In that same year Muhammad Ali beat Sonny Liston to become World Heavyweight Champion, Liverpool won the First Division title yet again and Tokyo hosted a highly successful Olympic Games. Outside sport, Nelson Mandela was sentenced to life imprisonment in South Africa and Martin Luther King was awarded the Nobel Peace Prize.

The 1964 Cup Final, featuring West Ham United and Preston North End, appeared as an anticlimax set against such seismic events occurring around the world. But this match was

*Ticket for the 1964 FA Cup Final.*

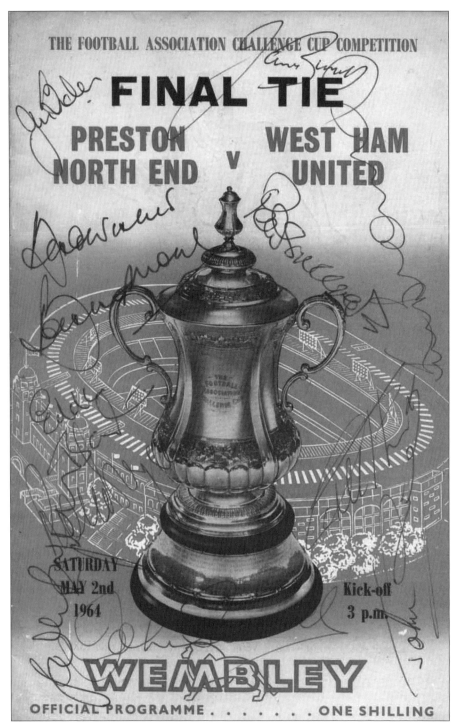

*1964 FA Cup Final programme signed by the players.*

no let-down. The game turned out to be one of the best Finals in the history of the old competition, up there with the great West Ham/Liverpool clash in Cardiff in 2006.

The Hammers' opponents were a modest Second Division side who had reached the Final with wins against Nottingham Forest, Bolton Wanderers, Carlisle United, Oxford City and Swansea City in the semi-final. The Irons had a more taxing path to Wembley but began their successful run with a routine 3–0 win at home against Charlton in the third round. The fourth-round draw saw neighbours Leyton Orient take the short drive up Stratford High Road. The Orient provided spirited opposition, but the Hammers controlled the game and ran out 3–1 winners.

The fifth round is not the place to start building up hopes that this could be your year in the Cup, and an away draw at Swindon had the ingredients for a classic West Ham banana skin. But, for once, a determined performance brought a comfortable 3–1 victory, and this time the dreaming could begin.

Reaching the last eight of the FA Cup gives a club's season real impetus and excitement. The level of expectation rose further when the Hammers were drawn at home to Burnley. The battle of the two claret-and-blue sides for a place in the semi-finals was greatly anticipated at Upton Park. As the teams came out, the atmosphere in the old Boleyn ground was electric. Bubbles could be heard out across the East End. The home team produced a performance worthy of the sixth round, winning by the comfortable margin of three goals to one.

The semi-final draw brought the opponents the Hammers least wanted – strong favourites Manchester United – but the tie has entered West Ham folklore as such a key match in the club's history that it warrants its own entry, as we have seen. The triumph over their mighty semi-final opponents found Hammers in the odd position of being clear favourites for the Final. The West Ham team was captained by the 23-year-old Moore, who had just been voted PFA Footballer of the Year, the youngest player ever to receive the coveted award. Moore had almost single-handedly steered his team to victory against Manchester United, and the Irons would need an equally classy performance from their captain if they were to overcome Preston.

The West Ham side contained 11 Englishman, the last all-English team to play in an FA Cup Final. Geoff Hurst was in the West Ham side but not the young Martin Peters, and the club's exciting young winger, Harry Redknapp, did not make his West Ham debut until the following season. Redknapp was busy making his name as a player of exceptional promise in the England side that won the European Junior Cup in Lisbon in 1964. Always true to his attacking instincts, Ron Greenwood opted for the teenage winger John Sissons ahead of Peters. With Ronnie 'Ticker' Boyce, Peter Brabrook and Johnny Budgie Byrne at the top of their game, this exciting West Ham team deserved to be firm favourites for the match. Preston would have other ideas.

The Preston manager was the former Liverpool midfielder Jimmy Milne, who included the young Howard Kendall in his side at the expense of the experienced

*Geoff Hurst (on knees) watches his header rebound off the Preston crossbar and over the line with goalkeeper Kelly's acrobatic bid in vain.*

Ian Davidson. Kendall, at 17 years and 345 days, was the youngest player to play in a Wembley Cup Final.

Preston settled more quickly into the match than their young opponents and had the best of the early exchanges. Kendall, Nobby Lawton and Alan Spavin were at the heart of Preston's best moves and helped their team gain control of midfield. Bobby Moore was content to play from a deep position at this stage, eyeing his lively opponents with some suspicion.

Moore had every reason to be concerned. In the 10th minute Preston took an early lead. Kendall and Lawton exchanged passes in the centre of the pitch, allowing Alex Dawson to fire a volley from the edge of the area, which the usually reliable Jim Standen fumbled. Outside-left Doug Holden was on the ball in a flash to put his side ahead.

Stunned by going behind so soon into the match, West Ham began to find their feet, and just two minutes after Preston had taken the lead Johnny Sissons raced down the left wing and played a one-two with Byrne before slipping a low shot past the helpless Kelly in the Preston goal. It was one all after just 12 minutes, and the crowd were heading for a pulsating Final.

Crucially for the Londoners, the mercurial Byrne began to assert his authority in midfield. A cult figure at the club, Byrne is generally regarded as one of the most skilful and influential Hammers of all time. He went close to getting the lead himself before laying on a good chance for Hurst, who uncharacteristically put his header wide.

Despite a period of intense West Ham pressure, Preston were always in the game and began taking control again as half-time approached. They also had two decent penalties appeals turned by referee Arthur Holland. With the West Ham fans looking forward to the interval, with their Bovril and hotdogs, Preston took the lead for the second time. Hammer's keeper Standen and centre-half Ken Brown got into a terrible tangle trying to deal with a corner, and Preston's burly centre-forward Alex Dawson was quick to take advantage, directing a downward header into the net. For the second time in the first half, the favourites found themselves a goal behind.

Half-time gave Ron Greenwood a chance to suggest some tactical changes, and, sure enough, his team came out for the second half quicker to the ball, adopting a much more aggressive style. Byrne was again at the heart of their best moves. Early in the second period the West Ham number nine hit a venomous drive straight into a very sensitive area of Tony Singleton's anatomy. Following treatment, the Preston centre-half recovered but was helpless to stop the Hammer's equaliser. Geoff Hurst levelled the scores with a header in circumstances that were oddly similar to his controversial goal in the World Cup Final two years later. Hurst's header hit the underside of the bar, rebounded from the back of 'keeper Kelly's head and trickled over the line. It was frustrating for Preston and was not vintage-Hurst play, but his goal brought the scores level. Now West Ham went for the jugular, and for the next 20 minutes they played the best football of the match, threatening to over-run the Preston defence.

First Bovington then Sissons and Hurst went close as the Hammers piled on the pressure. But, as is often the case in football, if a team fails to score when they are

*Ronnie Boyce (nearest camera) celebrates his winning goal in the 1964 FA Cup Final. Teammate Johnny Byrne also celebrates.*

on top, they run out of ideas and let their hard-won advantage slip. For the first time, the Preston winger Dave Wilson began to get into the match and run at Jack Burkett. The full-back was struggling to hold the youngster on an increasingly wet pitch. Meanwhile, the previously influential Byrne began to look weary in the difficult conditions. Midfield colleague Eddie Bovington was suffering from an attack of the notorious Wembley cramps as Preston began to pour through the Hammers' midfield. In what was becoming a titanic encounter, both sets of players hurled themselves at each other in an effort to gain the lead.

As the minutes ticked by, Preston looked the most likely to lift the trophy, when, as every West Ham supporter knew he would, Bobby Moore intervened to turn the game. Sensing that the game was slipping from their grasp and in a desperate attempt to inspire his side, the captain began striding forward into the opponent's half for the first time in the match. Moore began to link up with Hurst, and with the game deep in injury time, he found the West Ham number 10, who had set off on a run into the opposition half. Hurst slipped the ball out to Brabrook, who was free on the right of the Preston penalty area.

In a flash the Hammer's winger whipped over a cross to the far post, where Ticker Boyce arrived with perfect timing to nod the ball past Kelly and into the net. Ronnie Boyce was a hugely popular figure at the Boleyn, and it was appropriate that he scored the winner for his beloved Hammers. In truth, Boyce had redeemed himself in the final minute because, by his own high standards, he had been totally ineffective all afternoon. He had won the FA Cup for his club.

*West Ham players parade the FA Cup on their lap of honour around Wembley after their 3-2 victory over Preston.*

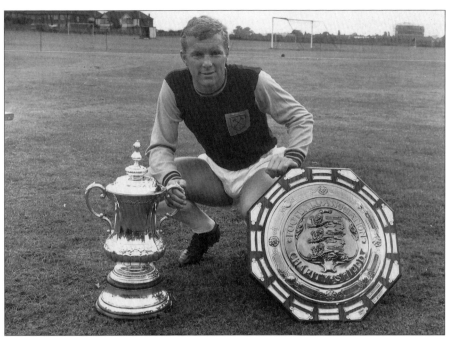

*West Ham skipper Bobby Moore proudly shows off the FA Cup and the FA Charity Shield before the start of the 1964-65 season.*

Bubbles resounded throughout the old stadium as Bobby Moore climbed the steps to the Royal Box to receive the FA Cup. He could not have dreamed that two years later he would take the same short journey to lift the Jules Rimet trophy for his country. The Hammers had won the FA Cup for the first time and were about to begin the most glorious chapter in their long history.

Celebrations went on long into the night in the streets of the old East End. The Black Lion pub in Plaistow was the place to be that night. The players regularly used the pub on weekends, and locals claimed there was an underground tunnel that linked the Upton Park dressing-rooms with the saloon bar of the Black Lion. Around 6 o'clock on Saturday nights, the players would be in the bar before the fans had made it back from the ground. The 1960s were a good time to be a Hammer.

Preston and their fans were inconsolable. They had dominated the match for long periods and lost in the cruellest manner – seconds before the final whistle. But they had played their part in one of the best matches in the history of the old competition. That evening Ron Greenwood would have asked himself why, after their commanding performance in the semi-final, did his team play so feebly at Wembley?

**Final score: West Ham United 3 Preston North End 2**
West Ham United: Standen, Bond, Burkett, Bovington, Brown, Moore, Brabrook, Boyce, Byrne, Hurst, Sissons.

# 9.

# WEST HAM UNITED
# V REAL ZARAGOZA

## EUROPEAN CUP-WINNERS' CUP SEMI-FINAL 27 APRIL 1965

The name Bobby Moore runs through the history of West Ham United like a soaring meteorite. It is difficult to think of a player anywhere who so absolutely defines a football club. He was captain of the Hammers through the most successful period in the club's history, while at the same time leading his country to glory in the World Cup. His peerless performances lit up some of the club's most memorable matches. It's almost as though the club was formed by Arnold Hills in the late 19th century just to create Bobby Moore.

In many ways Moore was a true Hammer. He never removed himself from his roots in the manner of today's celebrity footballers. Back in the mid-1960s Hammers fans could drop into Moore's pub in Stratford or see the great man in The Black Lion at Plaistow. The England captain and his first wife, Tina, could be seen most Saturdays nights after a home match in their local, The Retreat in Chigwell. Moore relished being a local hero, and he was always patient, courteous and friendly to his fans. From the terraces, supporters couldn't take their eyes off his play.

There is a photograph of Moore that beautifully encapsulates the man and the footballer. He is standing in the goalmouth in front of the North Bank at Upton Park, right hand against the near post, defending a corner for his beloved West Ham. His face betrays his feelings. His look is intense but imperious, displaying complete control of everything around him. He is entirely caught up in the moment – in his element and master of his all around him. Moore had supreme confidence, but this never strayed into arrogance. He always knew where he came

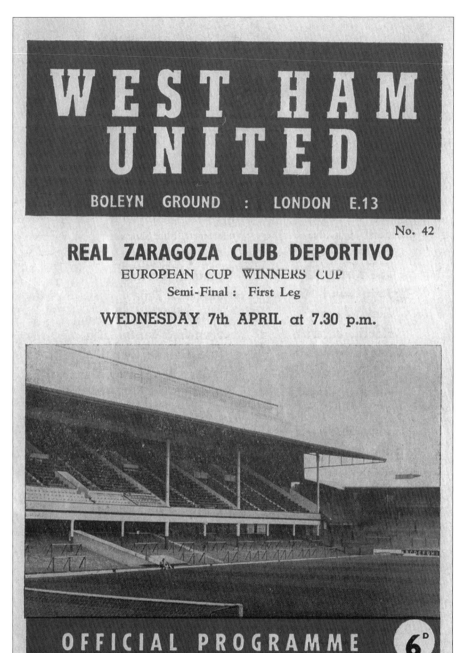

*Official programme from the Real Zaragoza match.*

from, and he was completely at home in the mud and rain on a winter's night in the East End of London, doing what he was born to do.

A few facts put Moore's achievement in clear perspective. He won two FA Cup-winners' medals and one European Cup-Winners' Cup medal, and the highlight of a truly glittering career was his World Cup triumph at Wembley in 1966. He was captain of the winning team on each of these occasions. Between 1962 and 1973 he was awarded 108 England caps, 90 of which were as captain. Moore made 544 appearances for West Ham and was the club captain for 10 years. Towards the end of his career he played 124 games for Fulham, including an FA Cup Final, ironically against West Ham United. He was Footballer of the Year in 1964, BBC Sports Personality of the Year and World Cup Player of Players in 1966, and in 1967 he was awarded the OBE. A BBC This is Your Life tribute followed.

There were hundreds of matches where Moore stood head and shoulders above any other player on the pitch. Like all great sport stars he was able to deliver his best when it really mattered. But two club games stand out, when his technical skill, football intelligence and sense of occasion came together in performances that were as awe-inspiring as they were effective.

The Hammers' passage to the semi-final of the European Cup-Winners' Cup in 1965 was not without incident; the club's fans would not expect anything else. First up was KAA Gent, who proved tough first-round opponents. The solid Gent defence frustrated the Hammers' forwards for long spells in both games, until goals from Brian Dear and Martin Peters clinched the tie for the East Londoners.

Sparta Prague provided less resistance in the second round, and suddenly the Hammers found themselves in the last eight of what was in 1965 a highly prestigious European competition. Quarter-final opponents Lausanne found the Hammers in fine form. Despite a few scares when Lausanne took an early lead in the home leg, a fortuitous own-goal and strikes from Brian Dear and Martin Peters eased the Hammers into the semi-final with a 6–4 aggregate win. Such giddy heights gave many fans

*Jim Standen punches clear during the European Cup-winners' Cup second-round second-leg game against Sparta in Prague in December 1964. The Hammers lost the game but won the tie on aggregate.*

West Ham United F.C.
BOLEYN GROUND, UPTON PARK, LONDON

European Cup Winners Cup
Quarter-Final Play-off
or
Semi-Final Tie

## WEST HAM UNITED
match
*(WHEN PLAYED)*

GRAND
STAND
15/-                    1965

| BLOCK | ROW | SEAT |
|-------|-----|------|
| E | W | № 14 |

*This portion to be retained as a PASS OUT*

*Ticket for the home leg of the quarter-final.*

a metaphorical nosebleed as they began to think the unthinkable. However, Real Zaragoza, the most feared team in the competition, were West Ham's semi-final opponents and stood firmly in the way of the club reaching its second successive Wembley Final.

The semi-final saw two wonderful nights of European football. In both games Bobby Moore's personal contribution ensured victory, but his performance in the second leg is said to have been the greatest game this magnificent footballer ever played. The Hammers were drawn at home for the first leg, which they narrowly won 2–1. Neither the fans nor the players really felt that a one-goal lead would be enough against a Zaragoza side with a star-studded forward line. The return leg in Spain turned out to be a classic.

The Hammers' defence began the game as they would finish it - penned back deep in their own half. The Zaragoza's famous five attackers grew increasingly frustrated as Moore and Ken Brown broke up their most promising attacks. But just as the away side's confidence grew, Real scored. In the 23rd minute Jim Standen beat out a vicious drive by the ever-dangerous Marcelino only for winger Lapetra to lash the loose ball high into Standen's net.

## EUROPEAN CUP-WINNERS CUP
## SEMI-FINAL 1st LEG

## WEST HAM UNITED
### v
## REAL ZARAGOZA

SOUVENIR
## PROGRAMME

*Pirate programme from the quarter-final.*

Sensing victory, Zaragoza launched attack after attack on the West Ham goal, with their wing-halves joining the forwards in the fun. But the Hammers' defence remained solid, keeping every defensive door and window shut tight, denying Real any chance of a shot at goal. As that doyen of football writers Ken Jones said in his Mirror article, 'West Ham defenders, led by Moore in resolute mood, sold every inch of penalty area space dearly.' Perhaps it was the thought of playing the final at Wembley later that year that so inspired Moore that evening.

Ron Greenwood had got his tactics just about right. He asked Ronnie Boyce to slot

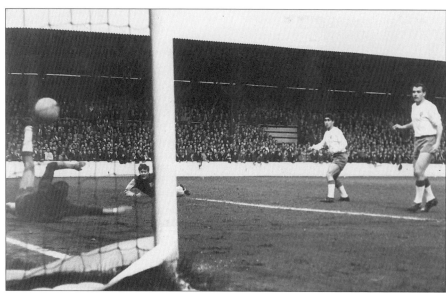

*Brian Dear, flat on the ground, watches his effort beat Real Zaragoza goalkeeper Enrique Yarza at Upton Park in April 1965. Hammers won this semi-final first-leg game 2-1.*

just in front of the defence, providing additional cover against the ever-dangerous Real forwards. Geoff Hurst was more or less left on his own up front, but he regularly tracked back for set pieces, where his powerful heading came to the rescue time after time.

Standen was magnificent in the West Ham goal, on one occasion contorting his body to pull off a breathtaking save against Marcelino, touching over a strike that seemed destined for the top corner of his goal. In front of him, Moore and Brown showed great physical determination not normally associated with a West Ham defence. Towards the end of the first-half, both players threw themselves into thundering tackles and blocked shot after Spanish shot.

In the 55th minute skipper Moore's heroic efforts were rewarded in the most unexpected way. Always calm under pressure, Martin Peters slipped a pass through to centre-forward Brian Dear, who, for once in the match, was deep in his opponent's half. Dear chested the ball down and, in time-honoured West Ham tradition, he slid a perfect through ball to John Sissons, sprinting in from the left.

Sissons tore through the Real defence, avoiding desperate challenges, before tucking the ball into the net with his right foot past the advancing Yorzo in the Real goal. John Sissons, a popular and talented outside-left, scored many goals for the Hammers, but none were as vital as the one he scored that night. It was a golden goal straight from the Chadwell Heath training ground, and it stunned the Real players and their noisy supporters.

In the closing minutes Real threw the kitchen sink at Moore and his defence, but they remained calm and grew in belief and confidence. They saw the game out without conceding a second goal, and West Ham United were back at Wembley for the second time in as many years.

Manager Greenwood said after the game, 'No one could be happier than I am tonight. Our tactics worked perfectly. We played the game without a centre-forward, and Zaragoza never used their extra man until centre-half Santamaria began to break forward in the last quarter of an hour.'

Moore himself revealed that the players were understandably edgy before the game: 'We put a brave face on it, but none of us believed deep down that that it would be enough. They called the Zaragoza forward line the Magnificent Five and we knew they would give us a real going over in Spain. Sure enough, they wiped out the lead early on and we were left trying to contain them for the rest of the match.' Struggling to hide his delight in the Hammers' performance, Moore continued: 'Suddenly John Sissons and Brian Dear broke away and knocked in a goal between them, and we'd got a great result.'

The Daily Mirror of Thursday 29 April 1965 carried the following banner headline on its sports pages: 'HOORAY! WEMBLEY AGAIN! Magnificent Hammers battle through to Europe Final.' This rather unrestrained notice heads a report of the match by Ken Jones. Jones described the Hammers' performance as a great display of discipline and bravery, and he suggested that the team's achievement demanded the greatest degree of dedication – words not often used to describe West Ham performances through the 1960s and since.

Greenwood's tactics undeniably played a part in the Hammer's two-leg victory. But it was Bobby Moore's stunning performance in the second-leg against Real's dangerous forwards that ensured his side reached the final. That evening the West Ham captain reached new levels of technical excellence, which he was to repeat for club and country time and time again as he approached the peak of his magnificent career.

It was not well-known at the time, but Moore had been diagnosed with cancer in November 1964. West Ham informed the press that their captain had picked up a niggling groin injury. Moore endured the treatment stoically, and he was lovingly supported by Tina, his family and friends. He returned to training in February 1965, regained his health and fitness, and quickly recovered his customary composure on the ball as he led his team towards the greatest prize in the club's long history. By the time of the Zaragoza match, Moore was back to his defiant and brilliant best. The Hammers progressed to the 1965 European Cup-Winners' Cup Final because, in Jeff Powell's words, 'the Magnificent Five had foundered on the Magnificent One'.

**Final score: West Ham United 3 Real Zaragoza 2**
West Ham United: Standen, Kirkup, Burkett, Peters, Brown, Moore, Byrne, Sealey, Hurst, Dear, Sissons.

# 10.

# WEST HAM UNITED
# V TSV 1860 MUNICH

## EUROPEAN CUP-WINNERS'
## CUP FINAL                              19 MAY 1965

In May 1965 West Ham United stood on the brink of creating history as the club prepared for the Final of the European Cup-Winners' Cup. From winning the West Ham Charity Cup in 1896 to a major European Championship in 69 years is a remarkable football story. The East End club was about to fulfill its destiny.

The 1960s were very early days for British teams in Europe, although Tottenham had won the Cup-Winners' Cup in Rotterdam in 1963. Expectations were not high as the Hammers fans wondered quite what to make of their European adventure, but it was a Cup competition and for West Ham, that meant anything was possible.

The club had finished ninth in the First Division that season and had their best group of players for many years, who formed the most successful side in the club's history. They had some wonderful footballers, like Johnny Byrne, Ken Brown, Ronnie Boyce, John Sissons, Alan Sealey, Jim Standen and their three great World Cup heroes, Moore, Hurst and Peters.

However, as Ken Jones pointed out in his piece in the Mirror the morning of the match, the club's achievements were largely ignored outside East London. They had been labelled as a talented team lacking the power and character to dominate domestic competitions. But Jones believed their football was fashioned for European success and the side's temperament had been steeled by a tough campaign that season. Jones wrote, 'I believe West Ham will win it...and convince the doubters of their greatness.'

The European Cup-Winners' Cup was second only to the European Cup in terms of prestige and honour, and this was the biggest club game that Wembley had

*Signed cover from the European Cup-Winners' Cup Final at Wembley*

*Ticket European Cup Winners' Final at Wembley*

EMPIRE STADIUM·WEMBLEY
EUROPEAN CUP WINNERS CUP
**FINAL TIE**
**Wednesday May 19, 1965**
**KICK-OFF 7.30 p.m.**
YOU ARE ADVISED TO TAKE UP YOUR POSITION BY 7.+.

CHAIRMAN:
WEMBLEY STADIUM LTD

**EAST ENCLOSURE**     **7/6**
ENTER **ENTRANCE**
**C** **13**    **STANDING**
TURNSTILE

TO BE RETAINED     (See Plan & Conditions on back)

hosted. It was also the first time that the BBC had been able to televise live an English club playing in a European final.

Claimed to have been the greatest European club Final of all time, West Ham certainly brought their A-game with them that evening. The Hammers' fans in the great stadium that evening would have been reassured by the sight of their captain, confident as ever, leading his team out alongside manager Greenwood. In front of a fiercely partisan crowd of 97,974, the Hammers settled quickly into the game. Playing their quick-passing style with a fluency and freedom that the Germans struggled to match, Moore's men began at a furious pace, pinning the Germans back in their own half for long periods.

After just a few minutes John Sissons missed a sitter from three yards, while 'keeper Radenkovic made brilliant saves from Brian 'Stag' Dear and Alan Sealey. But Munich had their moments in the breathtaking encounter, with the Hammers at their irresistible best. Both sides missed great chances in the first half, but at the interval the score remained level at 0–0.

The second half began at the same blistering pace before Dear went close again, while Sissons was desperately unlucky to hit a post. At the other end, Jim Standen needed to be alert as the Germans broke dangerously on several occasions, Kruppers and Grosser both testing the Hammers' 'keeper.

Gradually West Ham's more incisive passing began to take its toll, and Munich's defence struggled to resist their opponent's penetrating attacks. The decisive breakthrough came in the 70th minute, just when both teams were thinking about extra-time. The persistent Ronnie Boyce threaded a pass through the Munich defence to Alan Sealey, who crashed the ball gleefully into the net from a tight angle. West Ham had got the breakthrough – could they hang on?

Two minutes later the Hammers gave their answer when they went two up, sending the crowd into ecstacy. Moore delivered a searching cross into the German's penalty area, which Radenkovic failed to deal with, allowing Sealey to seize on a chance, easing the ball into the net, sealing the match for his team. The claret-and-blue thousands began to relax, and Bubbles rang around the ground.

Ken Jones was correct. Their final victory earned the Hammers praise across Europe and took the club to a new level. In front of a record Wembley crowd and an estimated 30 million TV viewers worldwide, West Ham became just the second English club side to win a European trophy.

*Alan Sealey is tackled by TSV Munich's Luttrop at Wembley during the 1965 European Cup-winners' Cup Final.*

Alan Sealey, a local lad from Canning Town, was an unlikely hero. Aged just 23, his two-goal burst in three second-half minutes grabbed the trophy and put West Ham on the European map. This year, 1965, brought mixed fortune for the young winger because apart from his historic Wembley brace he scored just three goals that season. The young winger got married shortly after the Wembley victory, with Moore the best man at his wedding. They were such good friends that the Moores even accompanied the newlyweds on their honeymoon. Everybody at the club, especially the fans, was delighted at Sealey's success in the most important game in the history of the club.

But a summer that promised so much for 'Sammy' Sealey ended in tragedy when playing in a friendly cricket match at the club's Chadwell Heath training ground. Like Bobby Moore and Geoff Hurst, Sealey was a decent club cricketer. Sadly, in this knockabout match he tripped over a wooden bench and suffered a broken leg. He struggled to recover from his accident and missed the whole of the following season, in which West Ham reached the semi-finals of the Cup-Winners' Cup and the Final of the League Cup. He was to play just four more League games for the Hammers.

If Alan Sealey grabbed the headlines, there are two other players who deserve a special mention for their contribution to the 1964–65 European campaign. Ronnie Boyce was West Ham through and through. A Plaistow boy, he made 342 appearances for the Hammers during the club's most successful seasons. Nicknamed 'Ticker' because of his ability to keep things ticking over in midfield, Boyce allowed the likes of Peters, Byrne, Sissons and later Trevor Brooking the freedom to get forward and support the attack. Not a regular goalscorer, Hammers fans will not forget Boyce's winning goal in the FA Cup Final against Preston in 1964.

After joining the club as an apprentice in 1959, Boyce played his last game for the Hammers against Leicester City in 1972. He played in all West Ham's finals in their glory years and worked as coach under John Lyall in the Cup Final victories over Fulham in 1975 and Arsenal in 1980. Boyce also worked under former teammate Billy Bonds before being appointed chief scout at Upton Park, a position he held until his retirement in 1995. Ronnie Boyce has a special place in the collective memory of Hammers supporters and is a true Hammers legend. He certainly played a key part in the final against Munich.

Johnny 'Budgie' Byrne missed out on the 1965 European Cup-Winners' Cup after playing a crucial part in the previous rounds. In a different way to Boyce, Byrne was at the fulcrum of the fast-flowing passing game encouraged by Ron Greenwood and later John Lyall. Unlike Ronnie Boyce and Alan Sealey, Byrne was not a local lad, being born across the river in Surrey. He earned the nickname 'Budgie' because of his non-stop chatter and bubbly personality.

West Ham paid Crystal Palace a transfer fee of £65,000 for Byrne in 1962, a record at that time. During his spell with Palace, Byrne played in the same England Under-23 side as Bobby Moore and Gordon Banks, and he represented his country at every level. As a youngster he looked a rare golden prospect, as good as they come. He duly won his first full England cap in 1961.

So keen was Greenwood to sign Byrne, who had struck up a good understanding with Moore in the Under-23 side, that he was prepared to throw the young Geoff Hurst in as makeweight for the Palace star forward. A few years later the whole of England had good reason to thank Palace for turning down the opportunity to sign the then wing-half.

Byrne played a few games with Jimmy Greaves in the England Under-23 side, and they immediately formed a dazzling partnership. In a match against Scotland, the London pair, both razor-sharp in thought and movement, continually tore the Scottish defence to shreds. That's how good Byrne was at the time; like Moore, Banks and Greaves, he was comfortable playing at the very highest level.

One of Ron Greenwood's most clever tactical moves was to convert Hurst from a rather ponderous wing-half into a centre-forward. Hurst was given a specific brief to take the physical weight off Byrne's shoulders. Ironically, the move paid off for Hurst more than it did for Byrne. But the partnership did reap immediate benefits, turning West Ham from a moderate, if skilful, side to real contenders in all the major competitions, including European trophies.

Byrne scored 33 goals in the 1963–64 season as the Hammers reached the semi-final of the League Cup and the FA Cup Final. He scored twice in the FA Cup quarter-final and played beautifully in the famous semi-final victory over Manchester United. But he saved his best form for the Final, in which his clever movement, subtle passing and delicate touches gave the Hammers the edge. His inch-perfect return pass to John Sissons, which freed the young winger to score the decisive goal, was a perfect example of his vision and quick thinking.

Johnny Byrne had everything – superb technique on a Brazilian scale, acute tactical awareness, and he was a natural goalscorer. He enjoyed an extended run in the England side but fell foul of Alf Ramsey's strict discipline. An England side containing Greaves, Moore and Johnny Byrne was always bound to push the boundaries a little, and it didn't help Byrne's cause when he pushed Greaves into a swimming pool during a team photo call. Ramsey would have made a mental note.

In 1964–65 Byrne continued to score heavily as West Ham enjoyed a brilliant run. His hat-trick in a 3–2 win against Tottenham in a thrilling local derby was one of the highlights of a sizzling burst of form. But just as he was beginning to reach his full potential, disaster struck when he suffered serious ligament damage playing for England against the old enemy, Scotland. In truth, he was never the same player again. He missed the Munich final with his place going to match hero Alan Sealey. Bryne's increasingly errant off-field activities and his damaged knee led Ramsey to omit him from his final 22 for the 1966 World Cup. This was a desperate disappointment to the players, the club and his fans. He seemed destined for greatness, but his career crashed and burned just as it was beginning to take flight.

In 1967 Byrne was sold back to Crystal Palace, but by then he was a shadow of his former glorious self. Ron Greenwood once described Byrne as the English Di Stefano, and a forward who had everything. He later added that he was everybody's friend but his own worst enemy.

Budgie Byrne played with a swagger and style, and as a footballer he ranked up alongside the greats. It would be kind to say that the awful effects of his injury sustained playing for England shortened what should have been a glittering career. Sadly, that's only partly accurate, but he remains a true West Ham hero and his play lit up Upton Park during the mid-1960s. Johnny Byrne died of a heart attack in South Africa in 1999, aged 61.

Byrne played his part in West Ham reaching the 1965 European Cup-Winners' Cup final, while the unsung Ronnie Boyce covered every blade of grass on the Wembley pitch that night. He was everywhere. The Hammers competed in a classic match, and, for once, they came away with the prize. Legendary sports journalist J.L. Manning wrote that 'it was not only a European Cup for West Ham but the best football match I have seen at Wembley since the stadium opened 42 years ago'.

The Hammers' captain remembered this moment in the club's history with typical understatement: 'We benefited from the experience of the previous year and took part in what many people believe was one of the best matches ever played at the old stadium. There was a lot of good football, and we played really well against

*Hammers players admire the European Cup-winners' Cup at the Chadwell Heath training ground.*

a good side with a lot of good players. We felt lucky to get the chance of satisfaction at Wembley so soon after the FA Cup Final.'

West Ham's victory over Munich was the highlight of Ron Greenwood's management career, and he later admitted his debt to his captain with untypical clarity: 'This was Bobby Moore's greatest game for West Ham. Technical perfection.' The normally reserved Hammers manager was heard to utter after the game, 'The match exceeded my wildest hopes.'

For West Ham fans there was a painful irony in that their best player did not have a happy relationship with his manager – Moore and Greenwood simply did not get on. The complicated relationship between the two men continued for years, and they never had the kind of bond at West Ham that John Lyall later enjoyed with Billy Bonds.

The frustration on Moore's part ran deep. He believed that Greenwood simply did not have the motivational skills and sheer determination necessary to be a successful, as well as principled, manager. Greenwood's insensitivity surfaced later in Moore's career when he was asked if he was sorry to see the former England captain leave the club. Greenwood answered coldly, 'I'm sorry when all players leave the club.'

Moore's irritation lay in his belief that West Ham had the best group of players in their history at this time, most of who were born locally. This team was good enough to win the League Championship, if Greenwood was prepared to sign one or two good players to strengthen the side. Rather bizarrely, Moore urged Greenwood to sign the aggressive but limited Maurice Setters to bring some much-needed grit to the Hammers' fragile midfield.

Moore believed that nobody had more knowledge of football than Greenwood, however, and despite their deep differences they usually presented a united front. After all, Moore could not deny his manager's achievements in the FA Cup and in Europe, but his club's commendable if limited achievements and their purist reputation were simply not enough for the ambitious England skipper.

Oddly, a further nine years at Upton Park slipped away after the FA Cup-Winners' Cup triumph in 1965 before Moore left the club. These were years in which the club seemed to lose its way. Greenwood's complex football brain failed to adjust the club's quick passing philosophy to meet the demands of the modern game's emphasis on hard tackling, uncompromising defence and direct tactics. This complex and decent man, a practising Christian, could not compromise, made poor signings and despised the thuggery and violence into which his beloved football descended in the 1970s, both on and off the field.

Moore left the club for a couple of seasons with Fulham before hanging up his golden boots. After his sad, early death in 1993 a statue was erected to his memory

*Bobby Moore shows of the Cup-winners' Cup at Newham Town Hall, assisted by the Mayor, Alderman Terence C. McMillan.*

at the new Wembley Stadium, and for most Hammers supporters, this was the most fitting and lasting tribute. The old stand on the south side of Upton Park was eventually demolished to make way for the new Bobby Moore Stand. As a further mark of respect, West Ham finally withdrew the number six shirt from the team numbers as a tribute to their greatest player, but not until 15 years after his death and after much pressure from the fans.

There will only ever be one Bobby Moore, and, to borrow an American phrase, if football was a song Bobby Moore would be the singer. The image of the blond-haired hero carrying the Jules Rimet trophy aloft on the 30 July 1966 is one of the most enduring, not only in sport but in British culture. Tom Geoghegan, writing in the BBC News Magazine, commented, 'Every time England crash out of a football tournament, the reputation of the late Bobby Moore is fortified just a little bit more.'

England's pitiful display in the 2010 World Cup in South Africa highlights just how low English football has sunk since that wonderful July Saturday in 1966. Moore relished the big occasion, while the England players of 2010 know only timidity, fear and defeat.

The European Cup-Winners' Cup victory over Munich remains the greatest moment in the history of West Ham United. As Moore climbed the 39 steps at Wembley to collect his second trophy inside 12 months, how could he have known that in just over a year he would back up those steps to collect the greatest prize in football.

**Final score: West Ham United 2 TSV 1860 Munich 0**
West Ham United: Standen, Kirkup, Brown, Moore, Burkett, Sealey, Peters, Boyce, Sissons, Dear, Hurst.

# 11.

# WEST HAM UNITED
# V SUNDERLAND

## DIVISION ONE                    19 OCTOBER 1968

Football was not always at the centre of the universe. In 1968 the world was engulfed in revolutionary fervour. In Paris, Rome, London and cities across America, young people took to the streets in violent protests against the Vietnam War and injustices at home. Great art is often produced in such times of brutal conflict and political turmoil. In England and the US in the late 1960s, we saw the greatest period of creativity in the history of popular music. The Beatles, Beach Boys, Rolling Stones, and The Who were at the peak of their creative brilliance.

The start of the 1967–68 football season saw an amazing exhibition of footballing artistry when the best Hammers side for a generation thrashed Sunderland 8–0, just down the road at Upton Park. These events were linked by a passion for creativity in the country that lasted a few short years before the violence and ugliness of the 1970s swept away the idealism of 1960s.

The West Ham team that season had evolved from the European Cup-Winners' Cup side of 1965. Gone were Ken Brown, Alan Sealey, Jim Standen, Johnny Byrne, Jack Burkett, Joe Kirkup and Brian Dear. In their place came a new generation of talented, mostly local lads, including Trevor Brooking, Billy Bonds, Clive Charles, Harry Redknapp, Alan Stephenson and a Scot, goalkeeper Bobbie Ferguson.

But there was only one hero on that Autumn day. He was a survivor of the victorious team of '65 and remains the only player in the entire history of football to score a hat-trick in a World Cup Final. A stunning performance by Geoff Hurst was the highlight of the club's record win in the top-flight of English football. Double hat-tricks have only occurred twice at the Boleyn in the history of the club. Vic Watson achieved the feat in the 8-2 home victory over Leeds United in a Second Division match in 1929. With the pitch heavy and thick with mud, we

# WEST HAM UNITED

**VERSUS**

# SUNDERLAND

FOOTBALL LEAGUE: Division One

## Saturday 19th October 1968

KICK-OFF 3 p.m.

No. 18

## OFFICIAL PROGRAMME 1/-

*Programme from West Ham against Sunderland, 19 October 1968.*

can only imagine the sight of Watson ploughing through the Leeds defence time and again as he crashed home each of his six goals.

Sixty years on Geoff Hurst repeated Watson's amazing feat with a clinical display of world-class finishing. It is fitting that Watson and Hurst scored the only two double Hammers' hat-tricks, as the prolific duo are first and second in the club's all-time list of highest goalscorers. Brian Dear did come close to joining Hurst and Watson's superb six, scoring five goals against West Brom in 1965. But as Hammers' goalscorers, Hurst and Watson remain supreme.

The carnival atmosphere at Upton Park on the day of Hurst's six goals against Sunderland was unique. In those days the Boleyn was a rickety old place with rusty turnstiles, tea bars, hot Bovril and the famous old Chicken Run. The local British Legion band entertained the crowd before the match, and delivered a passionate rendition of Bubbles as the teams ran out, one squad at a time. West Ham fans continue to sing Bubbles at the start of games, although some of the reggae or rap versions do offend the ear of older fans just a little.

Sunderland arrived at Upton Park for the match in a confident mood after a series of victories lifted them up to 10th spot in the First Division. However, the Wearsiders would still be smarting at the 5–1 drubbing at the hands of the Hammers at Roker Park the previous season. The home side were riding high in sixth place, but their most optimistic supporters could not have imagined the events that were about to unfold that Saturday afternoon.

As Hurst plundered a hat-trick in each half, the team put together a thrilling performance, which completely destroyed a competent Sunderland side. The purist ideals of Ron Greenwood and the creative planning of Cantwell, Allison, Sexton and others at the Casseratti Café came together in one match to produce perfect football – it was Hammer heaven that day.

The game started quietly enough as both sides took time to settle. Redknapp missed an early chance, and the deluge began in the 19th minute when Hurst dived to help Martin Peter's cross over the line with his hand. The home crowd were grateful for this slice of luck, and they began to relax when Bobby Moore hammered a 35-yard free-kick past Montgomery in the Sunderland goal. Moore scored a few goals for the club and always reacted in the same way, shaking a few hands and trotting back to his own half. Both the first two goals were received with calm dignity, in contrast to the madcap goal celebrations favoured by today's Premier League posers.

Hurst headed his second a few minutes later, following a quick interchange of passes between Brooking and Billy Bonds. Hurst completed his first-half hat-trick four minutes from half-time when he nodded in Harry Redknapp's accurate cross. It was Hurst's first hat-trick for over a year, and his team were ripping their opponents to shreds.

By the time the second half had begun, the atmosphere in the ground was riotous in the very best sense – it was party time at the Boleyn. The party really got going when Peters set up another Hurst goal. This time the striker chested the ball down in typical fashion before firing his shot past the helpless Sunderland 'keeper. On the hour Hurst smashed a 25-yard drive at the traumatised Montgomery. The ball took a deflection or two before nestling in the back of the net.

The sinewy skills of Trevor Brooking caused havoc in the Black Cat's defence, and the young midfielder notched his side's seventh goal later in the half. With the happy Hammers fans going barmy, Hurst, alive to every half-chance, scored his sixth as he calmly slotted in Redknapp's neat pass. The Wearsiders were dead and buried, and they trooped off at the end bemused and humiliated.

There were no more goals in the last 15 minutes, and the home supporters trooped home down Green Street and along the Barking Road having witnessed the finest performance by a West Ham side since the European triumph in 1965. Ironically, though, it was the club's lowest gate of the season. Hurst was given the match ball, which led Ronald Aitken of The Observer to comment the following day, 'Hurst was allowed to keep the ball as a momento, which was only proper since he had it for most of the afternoon.'

The match belonged to Geoff Hurst. The Greenwood-inspired transformation of Hurst from a wooden and pedestrian carthorse to the most dangerous centre-forward on the planet was complete. Of course, his greatest moment came in 1966, but the Sunderland match confirmed his elevation to superstar and West Ham legend. His cheeks puffing out with effort, Hurst brought running off the ball to new heights of efficiency. He led the line beautifully and ran the channels to great effect. His first touch was sure and surprisingly deft for a big man. Hurst fed hungrily on the skilful cleverness of Martin Peters and the young Brooking, and he got his head to the crosses of Sissons and Redknapp, who reaped havoc on the wings.

West Ham virtually invented the near-post cross. Perfect examples of this classic ploy were two goals scored by Hurst in the 1966 World Cup. The first was the only goal of the game against Argentina. For once, the number 10 got free of his marker and guided Peter's flighted cross into the far corner of the net. The second was perfection itself. In the final against Germany, Bobby Moore was fouled just inside the German half. The England skipper delayed his free-kick long enough for Hurst to complete his near-post run. The cross was so accurate that Hurst was able to guide his header easily into the net to put his side ahead. Both goals were straight out of the Chadwell Heath training ground.

There was no man in football more modest than Geoff Hurst. A consummate goalscorer, he ran his heart out in every match, but he would be the first to admit his debt to his teammates. It is worth giving a couple of them a special mention. West Ham's philosophy of football has always involved two speedy wingers deployed as wide as possible and with the ability to hit both near and fast-post crosses. Playing in the match against Sunderland were two exponents of classic wing-play, and both were perfectly attuned to Hurst's running and positional sense.

*Sir Geoff Hurst was just plain Geoff when he joined the Hammers in 1960. Six years later he was immortalised when he became the only man ever to score a hat-trick in a World Cup Final. Hurst made 499 senior appearances for West Ham (only one of them as a substitute) and scored 248 goals before moving to Stoke City for £80,000 in 1972. Forty-nine full caps brought him 24 goals altogether.*

The Hammers' outside-left that day, and for much of the 1960s, was John Sissons. Bobby Moore once said that Johnny Sissons kept threatening to be the best left-winger on earth. The skipper had a high opinion of the young winger, who had the sweetest left foot in the First Division. Moore recalled a match against Liverpool when the youngster ran Chris Lawler and tough-guy Tommy Smith ragged, despite being continually kicked into the Chicken Run by the uncompromising Scousers.

Older West Ham fans will remember that Sissons was the youngest player to score in an FA Cup Final. He also laid on the winning goal in the semi-final of the European Cup-Winners' Cup and, at the age of 19, played a vital role in the final at Wembley. He was quick, had wonderful ball skills and was the best trainer at the club in that era.

John Sissons should have had a long England career, but he never really fulfilled his great potential. As Moore said, 'He was a thoroughbred who never matured.' Despite this disappointment, Sissons was popular with fans, who remember his wonderful wing play and the crosses he supplied for Geoff Hurst.

After making his West Ham debut in 1963, John Sissons played 265 League and Cup games in his eight years at the club, and he scored 50 goals. He left the Hammers for Sheffield Wednesday before linking up again with ex-Hammer John Bond at Norwich City. He later became a successful businessman in South Africa, having enjoyed a few seasons with Cape Town at the end of his career. The part Sissons played in West Ham's glory years of the 1960s should never be underestimated.

One name that is unlikely to be forgotten or underestimated is Sissons' wing partner at Upton Park, Harry Redknapp. A fleet-footed outside-right, Poplar-born Redknapp made 150 appearances for West Ham between 1964 and 1972. Unusually tall for a winger at 5ft 11in, the tousled-haired youngster was a favourite of the Boleyn crowd, particularly the Chicken Run, who sought to protect him from the heavy challenges of opposition full-backs.

Redknapp was a real prospect as a youngster. He was outstanding for England Youth and was expected to enjoy a long international career. But, like Sissons, the young outside-right was considered a luxury player and was never really encouraged to fulfil his immense promise. Fortunately, at Upton Park he had the likes of Billy Bonds and Geoff Hurst to look out for him. His partnership with Bonds down the right side of the Hammers' attack produced some of the most exciting football by the 1960s side. Their pace and movement created chance after chance for Geoff Hurst, who must have loved having speedy wingers supplying him with tempting crosses. Fans have enduring memories of Bobby Moore driving a pass through to Hurst, who would chest it down first time into the path of Redknapp as he sped down the line.

No discussion of Harry Redknapp's time at West Ham can fail to mention his managerial career. It towers over his time as a player at the club. However, many of us prefer to remember the flying young winger in tandem with his wing partner, John

Sissons. The pair followed the tradition of great West Ham wingers and can be favourably compared with club legends like Eric Parsons, Terry Woodgate, Harry Hooper and Mike Grice.

Like most of West Ham's finest moments of the 1960s, Geoff Hurst was at the centre of the remarkable victory over Sunderland. It is unlikely that his double hat-trick will ever be repeated, as the club struggles to live up to its purist traditions. But for one day in 1968, West Ham reached dizzying heights of creativity that sat easily with the spirit of the times.

**Final score: West Ham United 8 Sunderland 0**

West Ham United: Standen, Bovington, Charles, Peters, Brown, Moore (captain), Brabrook, Boyce, Byrne, Hurst, Sissons, Burnett.

# 12.

# WEST HAM UNITED

# V BLACKPOOL

## FA CUP THIRD ROUND        2 JANUARY 1971

High-scoring thrillers, rousing, nail-biting cup-ties, games of historical interest or classics of breathtaking football are all ingredients that make memorable football matches. Or, as Harry Redknapp would say, make them different class. No account of West Ham's memorable matches can leave out one of the club's early, self-destructive FA Cup defeats. Swindon, Mansfield, Hull, Hereford, Stockport and Newport are all clubs who achieved feats of giant-killing at the expense of the Hammers. Most of these shocking results came in the Greenwood era, when moments of sublime attacking football were combined with defending that often bordered on the comical.

One of the excuses offered by the players at the time was the state of mid-season pitches. Mud, wind and rain worked against the Hammers' style of quick, inter-passing football, carefully built up from the back and worked through midfield. January pitches were a great leveller, more suited to the direct play of lower division clubs. If the team could survive in the Cup until conditions improved, then they had a real chance.

Such excuses never cut much ice with the fans as they witnessed their team caving in to yet another bunch of honest footballers determined to put one over on their soft-touch opponents. There is little argument about which was the worst of these miserable occasions. It was a match that is very difficult to forget.In January 1971, in the third round of the FA Cup, Blackpool inflicted on the Hammers one of the most humiliating defeats in the long and often distinguished history of the club. For supporters of a certain age the defeat still hurts.

When the third draw was made, both teams were struggling at the foot of the old First Division, but given the quality of the Hammers' side, Blackpool were considered as definite underdogs. Their new manager, Bob Stokoe, had only been

*Blackpool's programme for the game against West Ham.*

in post for a few days, and the club had been in disarray for some time. In contrast, the Hammers had the England captain at the heart of their defence, which also included Billy Bonds and Frank Lampard Snr. With a capable midfield featuring Peter Eustace and Bobby Howe, and potential match-winners in Jimmy Greaves and Clyde Best, it was difficult to see how West Ham could lose the game.

There were two things that troubled the fans who made the long trip north: the state of the pitch and the fact that Geoff Hurst was missing from the West Ham line up. The conditions were appalling. An icy wind blew off the sea, freezing the playing surface and the 22,000, mostly Blackpool, supporters who braved the elements to watch the match. To make matters worse, a thick mist began rolling round the ground, blown into Bloomfield Road from the sea beyond. They were perfect conditions for an upset.

The game got off to a tentative start, neither set of players able to find their feet in the atrocious conditions. The Blackpool defence was having the quieter afternoon, easily holding the Hammers' goal threat. Big, burly Clyde Best was never going to impress on the treacherous surface, but Jimmy Greaves, who should have made an impact, was quiet for long periods. Johnny Ayris, the Wapping Whippet, couldn't get going on the right wing and never worried the great Blackpool full-back Jimmy Armfield. Ayris had been a star at West Ham when he had made his first-team debut against Burnley in 1970. He was seen as a boy wonder, winning seven England Youth caps, but he never fulfilled his exciting potential. He made just 68 appearances for the Hammers before moving to Wimbledon in 1977.

With the Hammers' attack looking increasingly lame, Blackpool gained in confidence and began to dominate the game. At the heart of all the Seasiders' best moves was their talented inside-forward, Tony Green. He began to stretch the Londoners' defence by bringing Blackpool's two young wingers, Hutchinson and Burns, into the game. West Ham had two excellent full-backs in Bonds and Lampard Snr, but they struggled in the conditions against their quicker opponents.

Green seemed to have no difficulty with the surface, spraying passes around the pitch with ease, and as the visitors' defence retreated he began to carve them open with his pinpoint passing and clever positional play. Green was a huge talent, and it was a tragedy that his career was prematurely halted by a series of injuries. But even though Green was playing well, Blackpool needed to score while they were on top. On 30 minutes the inevitable happened. Again, the Scot ran at the heart of the Hammers' defence as they backtracked furiously on the treacherous surface. This time, as he reached the edge of the area, he slipped past Taylor and Moore and buried his shot low into the corner of Ferguson's net.

A few minutes later it was Green again who fastened on to a half-hearted clearance by Peter Eustace, and he fired a crisp volley into the top corner. Blackpool had been by far the better side, and they deserved their lead. They had mastered the conditions well and had the game's dominant force in Green. The Hammers looked all at sea and were lucky to go in at the interval only two goals down. Even the great Moore looked uncomfortable as he struggled to turn back the orange tide.

The hundreds of away fans must have prayed their side would come out for the second-half with a strong response to the sustained Blackpool pressure. If they didn't improve, they were out of the Cup at the first hurdle. The West Ham contingent might also have hoped that the inspired Tony Green would not come out for the second period, or at least stop looking like Pele on a good day. In the first half, with Kemp and Coleman, he wreaked havoc in midfield, and the Hammers got nowhere near him. The only player who looked remotely interested was Peter Eustace. The cultured number eight was signed from Sheffield Wednesday for £90,000 and stayed with the Hammers for two seasons. He was skilful but strong in possession. He just looked like a West Ham player, and it was a pity he came to Upton Park so late in his career.

Despite Eustace's second-half resistance, Green continued to run the visitors ragged and set up two early chances that went begging. Then he caught Bobby Howe dithering in possession, sprinted forward, rounded Ferguson and unselfishly rolled the ball across an empty goal to Craven, who belted it in from six yards. It was game over.

Late in the game Jimmy Greaves had a rare chance neatly stopped by Taylor's reflex save, but aside from that one effort there was nothing to cheer the Londoners sheltering in the stands from the biting wind. In the 80th minute Blackpool scored a fourth when Mowbray, up from left-back, smashed a short free-kick from Coleman like a rocket past a helpless Ferguson. Most Hammers supporters had left the ground by this time to make the long trip home to lick their wounds.

Blackpool had their day in the FA Cup sun, but they lost to Hull City in the next round. They were relegated at the end of the season after winning just one more game in Division One. Hero Tony Green was sold to Newcastle, where he was dogged by injury. He played just 220 matches in his career and only turned out for Scotland six times – sad numbers for such a wonderful footballer.

Meanwhile, the West Ham players trudged back to the dressing room to face the wrath of Ron Greenwood after being totally outplayed in every aspect of the game. Skipper Bobby Moore stood up and took the flack, and he was later referred to by Blackpool assistant manager Jimmy Meadows as 'the worst defender in the world'. Meadows later retracted his words and apologised to Moore, though this did not prevent his club sacking the coach for his indiscretion.

A few days later an angry phone call to the press by an irate Hammers fan led to one of the most shocking incidents in the history of West Ham United. It emerged that those old buddies Moore, Greaves, Brian Dear and Clyde Best had been seen the night before the match at the nightclub of former heavyweight boxing champion Brian London. The boxer was an old friend of Moore and Greaves, and, as they said at the time, 'We just popped in to see an old friend for a social drink – it was New Year, for goodness sake.'

Moore admitted the allegations were true and explained that the four arrived back in the hotel at 1.00am, perfectly sober, and ready to play the next day. Moore said later, 'We had a long and tedious train journey up to Blackpool. We had dinner at 7.30pm and heard plenty of people suggesting the next day's game would be off because the pitch was iced up.'

Moore had a couple of glasses of wine at dinner, and on the way to bed he bumped into Greaves, Best and Dear in the hotel foyer. They all decided to jump in a taxi and head down to London's 007 club, and, after a few beers, they returned to the hotel for coffee and sandwiches and were in their beds by 1.30pm. For Moore, Dear and Greaves, a few drinks before a game was nothing that unusual – this was a different time, and players were not under the constant glare of the press as they are today. As Moore added, 'We were in bed by 1.30 and got up about 10 o'clock the next morning. That's a good night sleep by anyone's standards…The problem was not the drinking. It was the result.'

Ron Greenwood felt more let down than angry about the incident. He was disappointed that Moore and Greaves had been responsible for leading young Best astray and were generally setting a poor example. The West Ham chairman Reg Pratt was not amused and believed he had little option but to punish the guilty trio. At the end of the following week, they were fined a week's wages and given a two-week suspension. On the Wednesday prior to the announcement, Moore was the subject for the BBC's This is Your Life programme; the next day he was a villain.

Both Moore and Greaves felt the punishment was over the top and that their main crime was in being caught. But whatever the rights and wrongs of the case, the incident had a major effect on the careers of the Blackpool three. Moore's long-standing dispute with his club deepened, and his golden image was slightly tarnished. Retirement for Jimmy Greaves came a year or two earlier than he would have wished, while Dear, with his social life and related weight problems, had been given enough chances by his manager. Moore, Greaves and Dear in the same side was really an accident waiting to happen.

Billy Bonds was in the side on that infamous day at Blackpool, and he first heard about the incident in the newspapers the following week. On the night before the match, Bonds and his roommate, Harry Redknapp, were watching TV quietly in their room, completely unaware that some of their teammates were out on the town.

Bonds later said that he never saw Greenwood as angry as he was that week and that the manager wanted to sack the players for gross misconduct. The full-back believed that players were wrong to be out before such an important match, but their behaviour had no affect on the way the team played. 'After all,' he said, 'there were seven of us who never went out.'

There is no question that the Blackpool affair left a nasty taste at the club. The fans were furious with the team for capitulating to a poor Blackpool side. Greenwood was deeply hurt by the incident, and the reputations of Moore and Greaves were damaged – at least for a few months.

*Bermuda-born striker Clyde Best scored 58 goals in 218 senior appearances for the Hammers after his debut in 1969-70. He left West Ham, his only League club, in 1976.*

The furore over the 007 nightclub fracas outshone what should have been a turning point in the career of Tony Green, who produced one of the greatest individual performances seen in the old First Division. It's a pity the West Ham players couldn't respond to his inspirational display – they would have had quite a game, and one that would have been memorable for all the right reasons.

**Final score: Blackpool 4 West Ham United 0**

West Ham United: Ferguson, Bonds, Lampard, Eustace, Taylor, Moore, Ayris, Lindsay, Best, Greaves, Howe.

Substitutes: Dear.

# 13.

# WEST HAM UNITED

# V STOKE CITY

## LEAGUE CUP SEMI-FINAL   26 JANUARY 1972

Some of the most memorable matches involving West Ham United have ended in defeat for the East Londoners. In the recent history of the club, European Cup ties and thrilling League matches against Manchester United and Liverpool ended in defeat. This is the way it will always be with teams like the Hammers. Supporters of the top clubs might expect their book of memorable matches to include only famous victories, but this book is more honest because these defeats, in their own way, were as memorable as more celebrated victories.

The marathon, twice-replayed 1972 League Cup semi-final tie against Stoke City was a truly epic encounter. Extremely tense throughout, the three clashes were as exciting as football matches get. They had everything, including goals, penalties saves, brilliant football from both sides and even a glimpse of Bobby Moore in goal.

The Hammers' team was almost as good as the trophy-winning side of the mid-1960s, although even a squad containing Moore, Bonds, Hurst, Brooking and Bryan Robson could only finish the 1971–72 campaign in lowly 14th place. The customary underachievement continued to infuriate the fans, who were hopeful of some Cup success that year.

Stoke City were going through an interesting period under manager Tony Waddington, who was in his 11th season as the club's manager. They were as inconsistent as the Hammers in the League but were famous Cup fighters. Waddington had assembled a mixture of youth and experience, bringing in quality players like Gordon Banks, home-grown defender Mike Pejic and the legendary pair Denis Smith and Eric Skeels. In midfield the tenacious Mike Bernard and John Mahoney balanced the skills of Peter Dobing and George Eastham, while in attack the dangerous trio of Terry Conroy, John Ritchie and Jimmy Greenhoff was always a serious goal threat. The ace in their pack was the greatest goalkeeper in the world,

Gordon Banks – as the Hammers found to their cost. Waddington had blended this collection of veterans and exciting young players into a team capable of winning trophies.

On paper the teams looked closely matched. Over the three games there was little to separate them as they traded blows like two heavy-weight boxers in the final round of a world title fight. West Ham were the more skilful outfit, bobbing and weaving and getting in close, while Stoke were all aggression and powerful hitting. If this had been a boxing match, the Hammers would have won on points by a clear majority, but they failed to finish off their opponent, who got off the floor to land the final and decisive blow.

In the League meeting between the teams, the match was notable for a Bobby Moore goal. How he must have relished scoring past the great Banks, his England teammate. Clyde Best also scored, and John Ritchie, one of Waddington's band of travelling soccer mercenaries, replied for Stoke. When the two teams were paired together in the semi-final of the League Cup, the North Bank began to dust off their old Wembley songs. Having beat Stoke comfortably in the League, the semi-final looked a formality. Some of the players may have taken the same view.

Stoke City had never won a major trophy in their 109 years of existence, and all the omens looked good for the Hammers. The first leg at Stoke confirmed West Ham's superiority and Stoke's vulnerability in Cup semi-finals – they had lost twice lost to Arsenal at the same stage in the FA Cup in the previous two seasons.

Peter Dobing raised the hopes of the partisan Stoke crowd of 38,000 when he put his side ahead in the first leg. The Hammers supporters feared the worst, but their

side gradually took control of the game, with Moore and Taylor in a dominant mood at the back and Brooking, Howe and Bonds outstanding in midfield. The Londoners got back on level terms when Geoff Hurst hammered a penalty past Banks in the Stoke goal. Hurst always had the same no-nonsense approach to penalty-taking. He simply ran up from the edge of the area and blasted the ball at the goal. It worked again on this occasion.

With the Hammers well on top, Harry Redknapp drifted down the right and sent a perfect cross over for Clyde Best, who made no mistake with his

*Programme cover from the first leg at Stoke.*

# HAMMER

### THE OFFICIAL PROGRAMME OF

# WEST HAM UNITED

# STOKE CITY

**FOOTBALL LEAGUE CUP: Semi-Final (Second Leg)**

## Wednesday 15 December 1971 at 7.30 pm

**FIVEPENCE**

28

*The home leg programme cover.*

header. Redknapp was in fine form on the right wing, enjoying the space that left-back Pejic was leaving behind him as Stoke pressed forward for an equaliser. With just the second leg at Upton Park to negotiate, the fans had every reason to believe their team was more than halfway to Wembley. The Hammers had worked hard for their 2–1 lead, and history was on their side as no team losing the first leg of a League Cup semi-final had ever recovered to reach the final.

Before the second leg, Bobby Moore had called for a real Boleyn welcome for Stoke. Moore got his wish and the noise in the ground was deafening as the players came out – the atmosphere in the ground was almost celebratory. But Stoke showed up at Upton Park in no mood to surrender. In contrast, both the fans and players of the home side may have been a shade overconfident and in danger of underestimating their opponents. But the match started where the first one left off, with West Ham dominant all over the pitch. The Stoke defence, well marshalled by Smith, managed to keep out Best and Bryan Robson, although both squandered reasonable first-half chances.

The second half followed the pattern of the first, and the match looked to be heading for a 0–0 draw, with West Ham back at Wembley for the first time since 1965. But gradually Stoke gained in confidence. They had defended well under pressure and now began to take a grip on midfield, with George Eastham giving an outstanding performance. The visitors' patience paid off in the 75th minute when they were gifted a goal. A rare mix-up between Taylor and full-back McDowell let in Dobing, who nipped in and turned the ball past the helpless Ferguson. The Stoke goal silenced the disbelieving home fans. Stoke were level on aggregate and back in the semi-final.

Then, in the 89th minute, in a moment of the highest drama ever witnessed at the Boleyn, the Hammers were awarded a penalty. Man of the match Redknapp had jinked past Pejic down the right side, had sped into the box and had been brought down by a heavy challenge from Gordon Banks – a certain penalty.

Geoff Hurst stepped up to take the kick right in front of the North Bank. You could have cut the air with a knife it was so tense. All Hurst had to do was convert the spot-kick and the Hammers were back at Wembley. There was no better penalty-taker than Hurst. He just had to repeat the one he scored in the first leg.

The World Cup hat-trick star and the greatest goalkeeper in the world up against each other with a Cup Final place at stake. The fans knew how Hurst would take the kick, and that was to blast it as hard as he could – it almost always worked. As the hero placed the ball on the spot, back in his own half Billy Bonds was crouching with his head in his hands looking the other way. Hundreds of fans in the

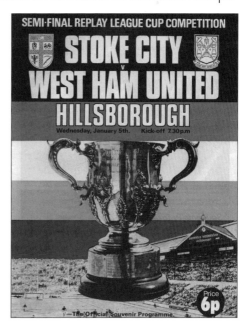

*Programme for the first replay from Hillsborough.*

North Bank couldn't watch either. Hurst took his normal long run and hit the ball with all his might just to the right of Banks. Somehow the England 'keeper got his elbow to the ball and it flew over the bar. Banks might not have known anything about the save – it just hit him as he reacted. But Hurst had missed, and the game went to extra-time. The North Bank gasped in horror as the ball flew high up in their stand, then fell silent as they realised what Banks' save meant to his team. In extra-time, as is often the case, both teams, perhaps numbed by the drama of the last few minutes, played cautiously and the tie went into a replay.

In comparison with the first two games, the replay was a dull affair and a real anti-climax, only lightened by near-misses from Best, which the incomparable Banks saved with ease. A 0–0 draw sent the tie into a fourth game and it had everything the first replay lacked – goals, mud, Bobby Moore donning the green shirt and an eventual winner.

Nearly 50,000 people crammed into Old Trafford for the second replay. There was a terrific incentive for both West Ham and Stoke. Not only did Wembley await the winner but also the chance to play Chelsea in the final, the Pensioners having seen off Tottenham in the other semi-final. The Hammers' line-up was the same, with Peter Eustace coming in as substitute.

The match started in the most dramatic fashion – it was pure theatre. Ferguson, the Hammers' goalkeeper, came out of his goal and comfortably collected a long through ball. Stoke's combative forward, Terry Conroy, thought he could get to the ball first, got it all wrong but decided to go through with the challenge anyway. The Irishman crashed into the Scot and laid him out flat. Play was stopped for at least five minutes as the West Ham 'keeper received treatment. He eventually got to his feet, but it was clear to everyone in the ground that he could not possibly continue.

Bryan 'Pop' Robson would normally take over between the posts in this situation, but his goal threat meant that Bobby Moore donned the green jersey. The world's best defender calmly took his place between the posts as though he had done it all his life. The Hammers got through the next 20 minutes comfortably until

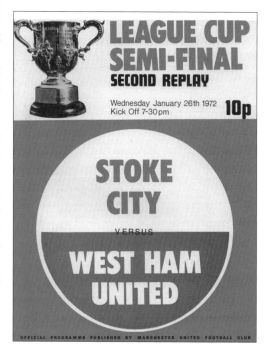

*Second replay programme.*

McDowell's under-hit back pass was intercepted by Ritchie. The West Ham full-back compounded his error by hauling the centre-forward to the ground, and the referee had no choice but to award Stoke a penalty.

The calmest person in the stadium at this critical moment was skipper Moore. It was quite a sight to see the great man in his mud-splattered green jersey, preparing himself to face Mike Bernard's penalty. Moore saved the kick, but the ball fell to Bernard, who gleefully smacked the rebound through the mud and into the back of the net. Ten minutes from half-time, and with a makeshift goalkeeper, the Hammers were a goal down and facing defeat.

This West Ham team had learnt from their humiliating FA Cup exit at the hands of Blackpool the previous season, and somehow they fought their way back into the match. Bonds took a return pass from Robson and hit a left shot, which took a deflection and wrong-footed the previously unbeatable Banks. Against the odds the Hammers were back in the tie and pushed forward for a second. Five minutes later, Bonds, deep in the Stoke half, crossed from the right into the path of Brooking on the edge of the box. Without hesitating, the number 10 hit a glorious half-volley into the net to put his team ahead.

Bubbles rang around Old Trafford as the Hammers fans celebrated what they thought would be a half-time lead. But Tony Waddington's Stoke were full of character, and on the stroke of half-time they equalised. Conroy, booed at every touch by the West Ham supporters, picked up a pass from Eastham and slid the ball through to Dobing. The inside-forward stretched for the pass and toe-ended his shot into the back of the net through a crowded and muddy goalmouth. The crowd were at once stunned and elated.

The Hammers fans were greatly relieved when Ferguson returned after the break to take his place in goal, allowing his skipper to resume his normal duties back in the heart of the defence. Despite Moore's reassuring return to the number-six shirt, Stoke began the second half much the stronger side. A long cross from Marsh was headed out by Bonds, easily the best player on the night for West Ham. Unfortunately for the defender, the ball dropped invitingly to Conroy, who promptly volleyed the ball over Ferguson into the net to give Stoke the lead. At this point Stoke looked the more likely to score, as they wore down the Hammers with their non-stop running and hard tackling. The sticky pitch negated the skills of Redknapp and Brooking, who were both visibly struggling as the game reached the last few minutes. Stoke were not to be denied this time.

Referee Partridge blew the final whistle, and after four games and 420 minutes of Cup football at its very best, Stoke City were on their way to Wembley to face Chelsea in the Final. The Hammers fans would have relished a London derby Cup final, but they had to make their way back to London comforted by the knowledge that, as Martin Godelman wrote, 'This had been one of the greatest English Cup ties ever played.' Underdogs Stoke went on to triumph at Wembley, beating a star-studded Chelsea team in the Final.

The Hammers had given everything in the four games against Stoke, and the fans had been magnificent. As they showed in this epic semi-final tie, this was a very good West Ham side. But following their Cup exit in early January, they limped along for the rest of the season, amassing a mere 36 points and finishing in 14th place in Division One. For one reason or another, manager Greenwood just could not get his players to a level of consistency that their ability merited. They fared better in the 1972–73 season and were to win the FA Cup again in 1975, but the thought remains that the team of the early 1970s underperformed.

There are players who are exempt from criticism, including Moore, Billy Bonds and the little goalscoring wizard, Bryan 'Pop' Robson. The diminutive striker was loved by the Hammers fans for his effort, understated ability and, of course, his goals. In his two spells and 254 appearances for the club he scored an impressive 104 goals. Robson cost what today seems a ridiculously low £120,000 when he was signed from Sunderland in 1971, but it was a record for the club at the time. He certainly repaid the money in full, scoring on his debut and regularly topping the club's goalscoring list. The fans showed their appreciation for the player they called 'The Bald Assassin' by naming him Hammer of the Year in 1973.

Robson played for England at Under-23 level but never gained a full cap. Billy Bonds said of Robson, 'The little fella was one of the best strikers I've ever played with and against, desperately unlucky to miss out on England honours.' Robson later regretted not staying longer at West Ham, and if he had there is no question that the popular forward would have made full club legend status.

In the semi-final against Stoke City, Robson was carefully policed by Denis Smith and his defence. The clash between them was one of the most important on the pitch, and Stoke won through to Wembley because they managed to stop the wonderful striker from scoring in all four games of the tie.

**Final score: West Ham United 2 Stoke City 3**
West Ham United: Ferguson, McDowell, Lampard, Bonds, Taylor, Moore (captain), Redknapp, Best, Hurst, Brooking, Robson.
Substitutes: Eustace.

# 14.

# WEST HAM UNITED
# V FULHAM

## FA CUP FINAL                    3 MAY 1975

In the wider world in 1975 the Vietnam War dragged on, the Watergate scandal threatened to bring down a President, the country was gripped by the Spaghetti House siege, the IRA blew up the London Hilton Hotel and the Moorgate tube crash brought tragedy to many East London families. On a lighter note, Ali beat Frazier in the 'Thriller in Manila', Leeds lost to Bayern Munich in a controversial European Cup Final, and, led by Brian Clough, Derby County won their second First Division Championship in four years.

1975 was a difficult year, but football remained as popular as ever, although the nastier side of the game regularly raised its ugly head. The FA Cup Final that year brought relief for two of the capital's less fashionable clubs when, against all the odds, West Ham and Fulham made it to the FA Cup Final. The old Wembley Stadium housed the occasion, but it was now a shabby and rundown apology of its former, glorious self. However, that would have not disturbed a single member of the 100,000 people jammed into the ground for the Cup Final of 1975.

Both West Ham and Fulham were real, old-fashioned football clubs. The Hammers were famous for their passionate support down in the East End and throughout Essex, although the glamour of the 1960s side was fading fast. Their opponents had a pretty riverside ground, but they were in the shadow of their trendier neighbours, Chelsea. The club could claim celebrity status through its chairman, Tommy Trinder, and in Johnny Haynes, one of England's greatest ever post-war footballers. Neither club attracted the media attention of Leeds, Liverpool, Manchester United and Arsenal, but both clubs had an abundance of characters. The 1975 Cup Final was one for the football romantics.

The clubs' two managers, Ron Greenwood and Alex Stock, were well-respected coaches who stood for the highest ideals in football. Greenwood, a practising

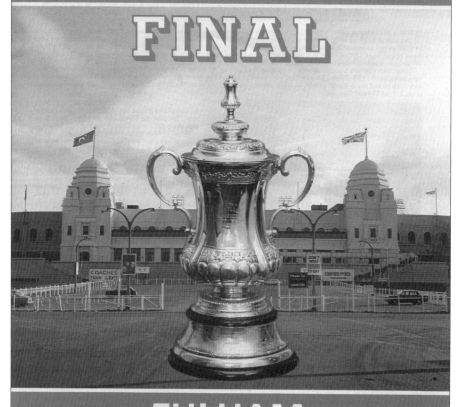

*FA Cup Final programme.*

*All smiles at the Boleyn Ground as West Ham pose for the camera before the 1975 FA Cup Final against Second Division Fulham. Back row (left to right): Robson, Best, Brooking, Bonds, Ferguson, Day, Lock, Holland, McDowell, McGiven. Front row: T.Taylor, Coleman, Gould, Lampard, A.Taylor, Paddon, Jennings.*

Christian, was the founder of Upton Park's famous Academy, and he later became the England manager. He had won the European Cup-Winners' Cup with the Hammers and brought the best out of the three great World Cup heroes of Upton Park. Stock, mercilessly parodied by Paul Whitehouse in The Fast Show, was less successful. But, despite his team being in the Second Division that season, Stock maintained his standing as one of the game's best managers, having coached such illustrious names as Jimmy Hill, Tosh Chamberlain, Bobby Robson and Johnny Haynes.

On the pitch that day were two former England captains, both on the Fulham side. Alan Mullery had been a magnificent player with Tottenham and England, while Bobby Moore, his incomparable colleague in the Fulham team, had not only won the World Cup for England but had been the most decorated and successful player to wear the claret-and-blue of West Ham United. The 1966 image of Moore lifting the Jules Rimet trophy remains as fresh in the memory as if it were 44 days, not 44 years ago. Now the great man was back at Wembley, sadly for the last time as a player.

Moore, as befitted his status, had a room of his own at the Fulham hotel in leafy Hadley Wood. The night before the match he slept well, and he set about calming his younger and more nervous teammates. He told the Fulham youngsters that West Ham were firm favourites, so let them do the worrying. His presence in the Fulham team was sure to give them an important psychological edge going into the game.

The sight of their legendary former skipper in the tunnel would be sure to jangle a few Hammers' nerves.

The 34-year old Moore made his own preparations before the game, his shorts going on last as usual. Firing jokes at the West Ham players in the tunnel, he strode out to take the warm applause of the grateful Wembley crowd. The ex-England captain played well, but he could not prevent the goalkeeping blunders that cost Fulham the game – 'bloody goalkeepers,' he said after the match. Later Moore must have looked at his losers' medal with a wry smile – he did not received many of those in his career.

Despite the romantic overtones, in reality the 1975 Final was contested by two moderate sides. Fulham were in the old Division Two, and although West Ham were in the First Division, they had managed to win only 13 of their 42 league games that season. But the fickleness of the FA Cup had thrown together two teams who, despite their modest form, had fully earned their place at Wembley.

The Hammers had seen off Southampton in the third round and Swindon in the fourth following a replay. The fifth round brought a routine home win against Queen's Park Rangers before the highlight of their 1975 Cup campaign, an impressive 2–0 win against Arsenal at Highbury. West Ham's name seemed to be on the Cup that year. A semi-final against a good Ipswich team followed, with Cup Final hero Alan Taylor scoring twice in a hard-fought replay. The Hammers were back at Wembley after a 10-year absence.

With three games against Hull City and four against Forest on their way to Wembley, Fulham had earned their Cup Final place the hard way. Birmingham City fought hard to deny them glory at the semi-final stage, but Fulham prevailed 1–0 in a replay.

As had become the custom, both sets of players appeared on the Wembley pitch an hour before kick-off clad in their expensive club suits. One by one they were interviewed for radio and TV. One player decided to miss the opportunity to answer mundane 'what's it like' media questions – Bobby Moore was nowhere to be seen. When asked the whereabouts of the great man, Alan Mullery explained he was having a kip in the dressing room. Clearly Moore wanted to save all his energy for the match.

West Ham supporters gave Moore a great ovation as the man who had brought such distinction to the club, and who was so shabbily treated by it, eventually set foot on the pitch for his final game at his beloved Wembley. The presence of Moore settled the Fulham side, as Billy Bonds predicted it would, and the West London team dominated the early part of the first half. A couple of powerful headers from Conway corners went close for Fulham before a vicious long-range Brooking drive grazed the top of the crossbar. An undistinguished first half left the Hammers supporters feeling anxious and Fulham fans expectant.

The West Londoners had every right to believe their team would win. A midfield containing Bonds, Brooking, Graham Paddon and Patsy Holland ought to prove a match for most top sides, but they struggled to impose themselves on lowly Fulham. There had been no sign in the first period of the classic passing game nurtured in

*Mervyn Day and Frank Lampard combine to thwart Les Barrett of Fulham in the 1975 FA Cup Final.*

the West Ham Academy. But as the second half developed, slowly but surely West Ham's class began to tell as they started to control the match for the first time. A breakthough now looked inevitable. and it finally came on the hour. Fulham 'keeper Mellor parried an awkward, dipping shot from Bill Jennings when he really should have held it. The rebound was gratefully crashed home by a lively Alan Taylor, and the Hammers supporters began to relax, if not yet celebrate.

Four minutes later their celebrations began in earnest as Taylor took advantage of another goalkeeping error to score a goal almost identical to his first. This time Mellor spilled a Graham Paddon screamer, and the centre-forward gleefully turned in the rebound. Despite Moore's courageous marshalling of his defence and Mullery's persistence, Fulham had nothing left. The two England captains were frustrated as they knew Billy Bonds was feeling his injury, and the Hammers' defence was there for the taking. Fortunately Frank Lampard Snr was at his very best, energetically covering his teammates and winning tackle after tackle. As the minutes passed the fans knew the Cup was well and truly on its way to the Boleyn.

Ultimately this was a pretty routine win for the favourites, and there was to be no dream ending for Bobby Moore, who slipped quietly away after the game, leaving West Ham to their triumph.

On the day two players stood out, and for very different reasons. Alan Taylor only joined the East London club from Rochdale in the autumn of 1974. Ron Greenwood willingly paid £40,000 for the youngster, who quickly became known as 'Sparrer' to his teammates. The 21-year old could not have imagined the fairytale season that lay ahead. He scored twice in the quarter-final against Arsenal and netted another two in the semi-final against Ipswich before his two Wembley goals ensured the 1975 FA Cup was adorned with the claret-and-blue of West Ham United.

Taylor's career soared like a meteor in 1974–75 as he went from Fourth Division zero to Hammers' Wembley hero in just a few short months. West Ham fans had every reason to think they had found their centre-forward for the next 10 years – here was the successor to Geoff Hurst and Johnnie Byrne rolled into one. Sadly, the Fulham Final was to prove the highlight of Taylor's career as he lost the golden touch of that season and it never returned. His career crashed and burned as quickly as it had taken off. But he will never be forgotten by the Hammers supporters for his exploits in their Cup run of 1975.

Patsy 'Dutch' Holland is one of the all-time favourite West Ham players. Blessed with neither the silky skills of Brooking nor the deft, dancing footwork of Devonshire, Holland had different qualities, ones which earned him the respect of his teammates. Holland used to visit school in the 1980s to coach promising youngsters, and the children adored him. He was always the most courteous of individuals and a tribute to his profession. Billy Bonds recognised Dutch's qualities and had a captain's respect for his midfielder. In his autobiography, Bonds wrote, 'Patsy was among the first I'd have wanted in any side of mine. He had far more ability than he was ever credited with. He could run all day.'

A key figure of the 1975 squad, Holland was left out of the side to play Arsenal in the 1980 FA Cup Final. Bonds did his best to console the distraught player, who was near to tears in the team hotel. But with typical generosity of spirit, Holland quickly recovered in time to cheer his side. The 1975 Final was the highlight of Dutch's career, as Cup Finals often are for players with his qualities of selfless running, decisive tackling and diligent marking. The nearest comparison for Holland is Alan Ball – he was that good.

Billy Bonds was another hero of 1975, playing through the pain of a knee injury and the discomfort of his recurring groin problem. Up in the Royal Box, Bonds raised the FA Cup in tribute to unsung heroes like Holland, but most of all to the thousands of fans celebrating below. The supporters knew they had a good side and were frustrated that the team had underperformed. The Boleyn faithful were desperate for success. They also knew the FA Cup provided their only realistic hope. This time they won, denying their greatest-ever player a fairytale ending to his stellar career.

This year did not see a vintage West Ham season in the club's great traditions, but a win is a win, and it was the FA Cup Final.

**Final score: West Ham United 2 Fulham 0**
West Ham United: Day, McDowell, T. Taylor, Lock, Lampard, Bonds (captain), Paddon, Brooking, Jennings, A. Taylor, Gould.
Substitutes: Holland.

# 15.

# WEST HAM UNITED

# V EINTRACHT FRANKFURT

## EUROPEAN CUP-WINNERS' CUP SEMI-FINAL, SECOND LEG                    18 OCTOBER 1976

The Hammers were in Europe for the second time in eleven years – their reward for scraping through against Fulham. Since that glorious night in 1965 at Wembley against Munich, the club had reached the semi-final of the Football League Cup twice, were beaten finalists in the same competition, and lost a European Cup-Winners' Cup semi-final, and, of course, won the FA Cup.

But the team of 1976 was a very different outfit from the successful, star-studded team of the 1960s. Moore, Hurst and Peters were gone, but in their place was the great Trevor Brooking and the admirable Billy Bonds. Alongside these two legends was a collection of solid professionals, who, on the 5 May 1976 found themselves in the semi-final of a major European competition.

After the hope and optimism of the 1960s, the decade that followed brought with it football hooliganism, industrial strife, punk rock, and, in 1979, a vengeful Tory government. The backlash was emphatic. Skinheads, with their Ben Sherman shirts, Doc Martin boots and racist sympathies, were the ultimate antidote to the 1960s idealism. The soulful, easy-listening of the Eagles, Stevie Wonder and Elton John was replaced by the shock of the Sex Pistols and punk rock. In many ways, the 1970s was a hard and ugly decade. The 1972 Munich Summer Olympics was ruined by terrorism, and it was a taste of horrors to come.

In football, the ugliness and violence spilled onto pitches in major stadiums and into streets around the grounds. Police dogs, baton charges and pitched battles between fans became commonplace. The results of out-of-control fan behaviour were wire fences, strict segregation and huge police presences.

# HAMMER

## OFFICIAL PROGRAMME : TENPENCE

EUROPEAN
CUP WINNERS CUP
1975-76
Semi-Final
Second Leg

Boleyn Ground
Upton Park, London
WEDNESDAY
14 APRIL 1976
7.30 p.m

## WEST HAM UNITED

## EINTRACHT FRANKFURT

*Programme cover from the 1976 European Cup-Winner's Cup Semi-Final.*

Sadly, West Ham fans were at the heart of the problem. Football-related violence in the East End began in the 1960s with the establishment of The Mile End Mob. During the 1970s the club gained real notoriety for the degree of hooliganism and aggressive fan behaviour towards their own and rival supporters. On one occasion, before a West Ham versus Fulham match, a gang of youths jumped on a Fulham supporter in Green Street and beat him senseless. His girlfriend cried in vain for help. This was at 2.00pm on a Saturday afternoon in broad daylight.

West Ham's Inter-City Firm (ICF) was a model for others to follow. They were highly organized and wore casual clothes rather than club colours to avoid police attention. They travelled to away matches on regular Inter-City trains rather than on the cheap and more tightly policed football specials. Their travel arrangements indicated that members were not the stereotypical unemployed youth of popular imagination but often city boys, skilled workers and even teachers. Films like The Firm and Green Street celebrated West Ham's ICF and brought the sheer intensity of football violence to the public's attention.

The Taylor Report (1991), following the Bradford, Heysal and Hillsborough disasters, led to the Premier League and the present day, sophisticated surveillance and policing. This, coupled with greater community involvement by clubs, has reduced the level of violence. There is one exception – the bitter rivalry between West Ham and Millwall remains as strong as ever.

One of the features of football of the 1970s was the loosening of the close bond between players and supporters. The warmth and sense of community of the 1960s, when the bond between players and fans was particularly close, weakened as players started to earn high wages and became detached from their fans and communities. This process reached its ultimate conclusion with the introduction of the Premier League and Sky TV. This was the background to top football in the 1970s, and we cannot ignore it.

Despite problems inside and outside the ground at the time, games under the Boleyn floodlights remained special. The return leg of the semi-final against Frankfurt was one of the most exciting, nail-biting confrontations seen at the ground in years. The atmosphere was electric, and the crowd that night were worth at least one, maybe two extra players. The fans knew only too well that West Ham didn't get these kinds of opportunities very often.

The route to the Final was surprisingly trouble-free, given that their League form was dreadful. They managed only one win in 21 matches between Boxing Day and the end of the season, leaving manager John Lyall totally exasperated by what seemed like capitulation. But this was West Ham – the ultimate Cup specialists. Their European charge saw them account for Reipas Lahti, Ararat Yerevan and, after a fierce encounter, Den Haag. Now only Eintracht Frankfurt could stop them reaching the Final for the second time.

In the 1976 side there were one or two residual elements of the triumphant FA Cup team. Trevor Brooking, Tommy Taylor, Patsy Holland and Frank Lampard Snr

*Trevor Brooking slides the ball past Eintracht goalkeeper Peter Kunter at a rain-soaked Upton Park in April 1976 and West Ham are on their way to another European Cup-winners' Cup Final.*

were local boys and remained close to their roots, and for most of the European campaign of 1976 the team consisted of eleven Englishmen, or twelve if you include substitute Alan Taylor. There was plenty to excite the supporters.

One thing different was the awful, bizarrely striped shirts the sponsors insisted the team wore. They were absolutely hideous and fortunately were soon replaced by more a traditional style. However, as much as the supporters hated the new strip, they put their reservations behind them on the night of the 14 April 1976, when Eintracht Frankfurt arrived to play the second leg of the quarter-final tie. Over 39,000 crammed into the Boleyn that night. Fans ignored the torrential rain and raised the roof of the old stadium in support of their side. Never in the club's history could Bubbles be heard so long and so loud. By the end of the match everyone in the ground was soaked to the skin, but what a night!

The Germans came to Upton Park with a slender one-goal advantage after their 2–1 victory in Frankfurt. Graham Paddon gave the Hammers the lead in the first game with a spectacular and precious away goal, only for the home side to gain the advantage with goals from Neuberger and Kraus. But there was everything to play for in the second leg.

As the teams made their entrance, they were greeted with a deafening roar from the home crowd that lasted throughout the night. The football matched the atmosphere as the Hammers rained down on the German goal in a desperate bid to level the scores. Lampard Snr, driving forward from left-back, twice went close, while in the 15th minute, Keith Robson had what looked like a good goal disallowed for a foul on the goalkeeper. For all the passion in the ground and all the efforts of the players, the Hammers could not get the breakthrough, and the interval came with the aggregate score unchanged.

We will never know what John Lyall said to his players at half-time, but with the crowd notching up the sound to previously unheard levels, the home team came out for the second half and battered the German defence. A few minutes into the second half the Hammers achieved the breakthrough they desperately needed. In typical fashion, Lampard tore down the left wing, to the delight of the Chicken Run, before sending a perfect cross into the path of Brooking. The midfielder, not known for his heading ability, sent a looping header over the German 'keeper into the net, right in front of the South Bank. With Paddon's away goal, the Hammers were effectively a goal ahead on aggregate.

Everyone knew the Germans would fight back. Mervyn Day had to be on his toes to keep out a shot from Wenzel, and Coleman cleared off the line as Frankfurt began to stretch the Hammers' defence. Fortunately for the home side, Billy Bonds was in inspirational form, and Paddon, Brooking and Patsy Holland worked tirelessly alongside their skipper in midfield. The Hammers were fighting to maintain their lead and were playing with real purpose and skill. Brooking and Holland were trying to support Jennings and Robson at every opportunity. All this led to tremendously exciting end-to-end football. The players and supporters were aware that a one-goal lead would probably not be enough against this German side.

Midway through the second half Brooking, who was beginning to dominate the midfield despite the thick mud, slipped a peach of a ball through to Robson, whose poor first touch brought groans from the crowd. The combative forward quickly recovered and curled a 25-yard shot over Kunter in the German goal, destroying the German fierce resistance.

Day turned a ferocious shot from Grabowski over his crossbar before Brooking brought everyone in the ground to their feet with a goal of his own. This time Paddon released his midfield partner, who jinked past two defenders before calmly sliding the ball into the net. The Hammers had a 3–0 lead and surely a place in the Final. The Germans never know when they are beaten and scored a very late goal, but it was too little, too late, and when the referee blew for time the home side were through 4–3 on aggregate.

In conditions not suited to his close control and stylish play, Brooking was at his brilliant best all evening. After the match he remarked, 'To score twice and set one up for "Mad Robbo" in such a key match was fantastic. Eintracht were a very good side and it all got a bit gritty in the end.' In a tribute to the supporters, goalscorer Robson commented, 'Our great crowd were worth a goal...we were elated to hear the final whistle. That was the greatest night of my life.'

It was a night when the team of the mid-1970s at last played to their full potential, but it needed Brooking and his friend Billy Bonds to be at their very best and the rest of the team to be 100% committed. Skipper Bonds said about his friend's performance that night, 'Trevor played many fine games in his career, but if I had to name just one as his best, it was that electric night. He was sheer brilliance. He mesmerised a good German side and scored two goals.'

For once, thanks to the crowd's noisy support, the performance matched the potential. Manager Lyall was delighted with his side's display on the night, but he must have been left wondering how on earth they had failed to win a League game since 24 January. But for now, they were in the European Cup-Winners' Cup Final for the second time in their history.

**Final score: West Ham United 4 Eintracht Frankfurt 2**
West Ham United: Day, McDowell, Lampard, Taylor, Coleman, Holland, Brooking, Bonds, Paddon, Robson, Jennings.

# 16.

# WEST HAM UNITED

# V ANDERLECHT

## EUROPEAN CUP-WINNERS'

## CUP FINAL                                    5 MAY 1976

The 1976 European Cup-Winners' Cup Final between West Ham and Anderlecht was mercifully free of violence and antagonism between the two sets of fans. The match was played at the Heysel Stadium in Brussels in front of 51,000 passionate but respectful supporters. Anderlecht began with a real advantage as Brussels was their home city. Billy Bonds likened his team's task to playing Liverpool at Anfield, even though the opposition's home ground was actually down the road in another part of town.

How frustrating it must have been for Irons supporters to see a team that included Brooking, Frank Lampard Snr, Billy Bonds and Tommy Taylor struggle in the League. But the Hammers were in their second European Final in eleven seasons, and who knew what might happen. They would need to repeat their outstanding form against Frankfurt on that wonderful night at Upton Park if they were to win the coveted trophy for the second time.

West Ham's Belgian opponents were a very good side indeed. Anderlecht had reached the Final after games against Rapid Bucharest, Borac Banja Luka, Wrexham and Sachsenring. The Anderlecht team contained some illustrious names, including Robbie Rensenbrink, Francois Van der Elst and the wonderfully talented Arie Haan. These players were highly skilled and experienced in top European competitions. They played a typical possession game, were comfortable on the ball and could pass and move at bewildering speed. The Hammers needed to be at their very best that night just to compete with the Belgians.

The Hammers started the game well and pressed Anderlecht back into their half. The Belgian's defence had not conceded a goal at home throughout the

**1975/76**

EUROPEAN CUPWINNERS CUP
COUPE D'EUROPE DES VAINQUEURS DE COUPE
EUROPABEKER DER BEKERWINNAARS

FIN.
5.5.1976 (20)
ST. HEYSEL

# R.S.C.
# Anderlechtois

# West Ham
# United

PROGRAMME : 25 F.

*1976 European Cup-Winner's Cup Final programme cover.*

competition, and it would need a moment of real inspiration to break them down. In the 28th minute the Hammers found a way through and scored from an unlikely source. The vastly underrated Patsy Holland put his side ahead with a well-hit left-foot shot that left the Belgian 'keeper helpless. The midfielder later revealed, 'I just hadn't been able to get into the game, but then I gambled that I would get on to a Bonds flick-on, and Bob's your uncle, I caught the ball perfectly with my rarely used left foot and put us ahead.'

Holland was a wonderful player for the Hammers. A tricky winger or box-to-box midfield player, he was respected by his teammates for his endless running and total commitment to his team. He was never really accepted by the fans, who failed to appreciate his value to the side. Billy Bonds rated Patsy Holland very highly: 'He had far more ability than he was ever credited with and, even more important, never hid when the going got tough. Patsy was always the first I'd want in my side.'

A serious injury from which he never really recovered shortened Holland's career, but his goals and his courage will not be forgotten by those who followed the Hammers during the 1970s. Patsy made nearly 300 League and Cup appearances for the club. He later went into coaching and club management, and he is now chief scout at Milton Keynes Dons under Paul Ince and runs a successful wine bar in Essex. Holland is good man who deserved every good thing that came his way.

Stunned by Holland's goal, Anderlecht ran out of ideas for a spell, but just when the Hammers looked to be heading for the interval a goal ahead, the ever-dangerous Belgians equalized. In the dying minutes of the first half, Trevor Brooking crashed a shot against the bar. Anderlecht broke forward from the rebound. Always dependable, Frank Lampard Snr stopped the attack, and in an attempt to slide the ball back to Mervyn Day he tripped and twisted his knee. Peter Ressel was on it in a flash. Punishing the full-back's error, Ressel slipped the ball to Robbie Rensenbrink, who scored with ease. Brooking said after the game, 'We had been playing well. Then poor Frank Lampard caught his stud in the turf and injured himself trying to pass the ball back to Mervyn Day and they got an equaliser.' The goal proved to be the major turning point in the match.

Encouraged by their stroke of luck before the break, Anderlecht began the second half strongly, and their fast-flowing football threatened to overwhelm the Hammers' defence. Then the inevitable happened and the Belgians took the lead with a well-taken goal by Van der Elst.

The talented Belgian later joined West Ham from New York Cosmos, and Frankie, as he became known at the club, had everything – pace, skill and the ability to score goals. Sadly, he found it difficult to adjust to the physical demands of the English game, although he did score some memorable goals for the Hammers, including a hat-trick against Notts County. But Frankie was better suited to international football, with its emphasis on passing, movement and individual skill, and he continued to perform well for his country. He was very popular with the rest of the players at the club and was one of the Hammers' better foreign signings.

Van der Elst, Rensenbrink and Arie Hann began to play scintillating football and slaughtered the Hammers for the best part of 30 minutes before the London side conjured up an equaliser out of nowhere. In the 69th minute Brooking, by now struggling with a groin injury, curled in a speculative low cross, which Keith Robson got to first and turned the ball into the net with a neat, low header. Somehow the Hammers were back in the match.

But in this see-saw encounter, the away fans hopes of a recovery were soon scuppered. Rensenbrink scored from the penalty spot in the 73rd minute, after being hauled down in the box by Pat Holland. The winger was appalled by the decision: 'No, it wasn't a penalty because I got the ball before he went down...Robbie just got up and didn't even appeal but somehow the referee gave it.

It certainly wasn't an obvious penalty, but the Hammers were 3–1 down with only 10 minutes remaining. There was to be no reprieve as Anderlecht continued to dominate play. The Belgians, in total control, waited patiently for their moment. It came in the 88th minute, when Van der Elst raced clear of the tiring Hammers defence and slipped the ball passed Day to seal a 4–2 victory.

At the final whistle a distraught Keith Robson, not normally an emotional footballer, had to be dissuaded from refusing to accept his runners'-up medal. He said at the time, 'I may have scored in the Final, but that defeat destroyed me. After beating Eintracht, we were probably a bit too confident. We had done so much to get there, but we made too many mistakes and, in the end, we just gave it away.' In truth, Anderlecht were a joy to watch in the second half and were far too good for the Hammers, who had two of their best players, Brooking and Lampard, struggling with injuries. Skipper Bond, honest to a fault, summed up the game: 'We could have no complaints; the better team on the night won.'

For the Hammers' skipper the Anderlecht match had very mixed memories. Bond wrote in his autobiography, 'It should have been the high point of my life, leading the Hammers in a European Final.' The reality for Bonds was very different. His wife's mother had been taken seriously ill and he considered pulling out of the match, but he was persuaded to play by his wife, Lyn, and his father-in-law. The team flew out on the Monday that week, but Bonds travelled out later on the Supporters' Club flight from Luton. Given the circumstances, Bonds played well in the Final, but he never really had a bad game? Rather than attend the post-match reception he flew straight home and found his wife in tears. Her mother had passed away during the night.

The fans were not aware of their captain's problems that night, but the 1976 European Cup Final was largely an anticlimax for the Boleyn faithful. But they could return to England once again proud of their performance in Europe. Their League position was a different story. but as Trevor Brooking reminded us, 'We may have only been a little East London club, but right from the 1960s, Ron Greenwood – and then John Lyall – imposed a philosophy at West Ham that meant we could adapt to a European style and cope at a higher technical level.'

Most Hammers fans would agree that the team of the 1970s failed to live up to the standards set by Bobby Moore's victorious side. They did win the FA Cup in 1975 and had two decent runs in Europe, but the glory days were over. Being West Ham, there were moments of triumph and disaster to come in the years ahead. The first of these came in 1978, when the club was relegated from the old First Division. They bounced back in 1981, when the Greenwood/Lyall dynasty was almost over.

In Billy Bonds and Trevor Brooking, West Ham had two of the best players in England. The swashbuckling Hammers captain, with his beard and flowing hair, was an inspiration and the fans loved him because of his total commitment to the club. Bonds played 793 games for the Hammers between 1967 and 1988 – a club record that is unlikely to beaten. His greatest disappointment was not losing at Heysel or frustration at his team's poor League form, but never winning a full England cap. He was selected for the national squad three times by Ron Greenwood, ironically the England boss at the time. But, due to injury, the only time he pulled on an England shirt was as an unused substitute In a match against Italy. When you consider the second-rate players selected by successive national managers during Bonds' career, it is nothing short of outrageous that he didn't win at least 50 caps. He will hate being labelled like this, but he surely must have been the best player never to win a full cap for his country. Bonds is a god at Upton Park, the word legend doesn't quite do it.

Bonds was awarded the MBE in the 1987 New Year's Honours List for his services to football. It was the proudest day of his life, and no one deserved it more. He received hundreds of letters of congratulation, including one from Kenny Dalglish, who wrote fondly, 'Congratulations. Now you've got an MBE, isn't it time you packed it in?'

Bonds and Trevor 'Boog' Brooking were best friends and roommates. When they retired from the professional game they played together for an Essex Sunday league side. They would have felt bitter disappointment at losing to Anderlecht, but their greatest moment playing for West Ham was still to come.

The team of 1976 enjoyed a wonderful European Cup campaign, but with Lampard and Brooking struggling with injuries in the final, the match at the Heysel was a step too far for Bonds and his men.

**Final score: Anderlecht 4 West Ham United 2**
West Ham United: Day, Coleman, Bonds, T. Taylor, Lampard, McDowell, Brooking, Paddon, Holland, Jennings, Robson.
Substitutes: A. Taylor.

# 17.

# WEST HAM UNITED
# V ARSENAL

## FA CUP FINAL                    10 MAY 1980

In May 1980 Margaret Thatcher had been Prime Minister for just 12 months, Dexy's Midnight Runners were number one in the charts and violence and hooliganism continued to blight English football. Upton Park on match days was a dangerous place, with pitched battles at local underground stations, dozens of police dogs shepherding fans to and from the ground, and barbed-wire fences separating rival supporters. The North Bank's Inter-City Firm (ICF) was among the most notorious perpetrators of football violence. The Taylor Report and the glamour of the Premier League were still 12 years away. But some things never change as Liverpool won the First Division Championship by two points from Manchester United.

None of this mattered for the 100,000 people in the ground on a gorgeous day in early May. For West Ham fans, beating Arsenal in an FA Cup Final at Wembley is about as good as it gets. The club had won the FA Cup on two previous occasions, but the 1980 Final was very special and has a remained vivid memory in the collective consciousness of the East London club. For those old enough and fortunate enough to have been at the old stadium on that sunny spring Saturday, the memory is simply unforgettable.

By the club's own erratic standards, the route to Wembley was uncharacteristically smooth, at least up until the semi-final. After coming out on top after a third-round replay

*Ticket for the 1980 FA Cup Final.*

**THE EMPIRE STADIUM, WEMBLEY**
The Football Association No ticket genuine unless it carries a Lion's Head watermark below
**Challenge Cup Competition**
## FINAL TIE
**SAT., MAY 10, 1980**
KICK-OFF 3.00 p.m.
YOU ARE ADVISED TO TAKE UP
YOUR POSITION BY 2.30p.m.
1. This ticket is not transferable.
2. This counterfoil must be re-tained for at least 6 months.
*J.S.Lill* CHAIRMAN: WEMBLEY STADIUM LTD
STANDING
£3.50
TO BE RETAINED        SEE PLAN AND CONDITIONS ON BACK
TURNSTILES
**C**
ENTRANCE
**10**
**EAST**
**UPPER STANDING ENCLOSURE**
19

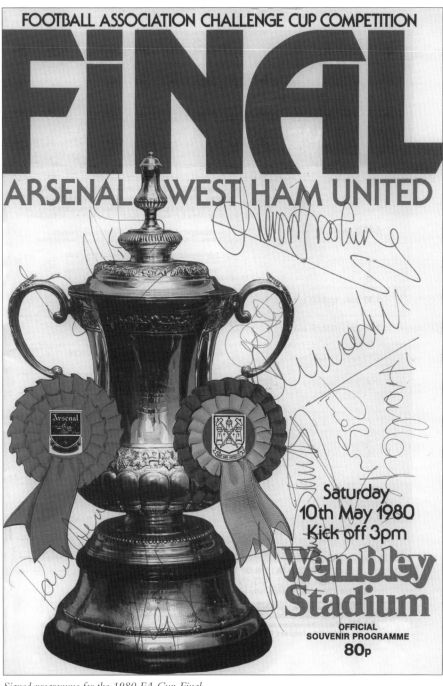

*Signed programme for the 1980 FA Cup Final.*

against West Brom 2–1, neighbours Orient were seen off 3–2 at Brisbane Road. The Hammers had got through their normal post-Christmas vulnerability and could look forward to the improved spring surfaces with confidence. The fifth and sixth-round ties brought confident home wins at the expense of Swansea and Aston Villa respectively, and the fans could begin to hope. The Hammers earned their place at Wembley following a hard-fought semi-final dual with Everton, winning 2–1 in a replay.

The semi-final against Everton will be best remembered by West Ham fans for the winning late goal by Frank Lampard Snr from a diving header. His outrageous celebration routine of sprinting to the West Ham fans before dancing an improbable jig around the nearest corner flag remains clear in the mind. But surely the man of the match was Alan Devonshire. The elegant midfielder played some exquisite football with Brooking, some of the best ever seen at Upton Park. Devonshire, a cult figure at the club, dominated the midfield that day and scored an unforgettable goal, beating what seemed like the whole Everton team before sliding the ball past the helpless Everton 'keeper.

Wembley opponents Arsenal reached the Final after four exhausting and bone-crunching games against the mighty Liverpool. Many neutral observers and commentators wanted an Arsenal/Liverpool Final that year and were disappointed when the two First Division bitter rivals were drawn together in the semis.

The 1980 Final was the 99th to be played at Wembley Stadium. The Hammers had reached the Final on five occasions, while their illustrious North London neighbours had contested the previous two finals and were a formidable First Division side. Although most Hammers supporters accepted their team was a huge underdog, skipper Billy Bonds had other ideas: 'We didn't really go into the game thinking we were underdogs because, although we were a Second Division side, we had a lot of very good players in the team. If you look at that team a lot of them became legends at the club.'

Bonds had a point. You could reel off the names: Trevor Brooking, Phil Parkes, Frank Lampard, Alvin Martin, Alan Devonshire, and of course, Bonds himself. The fans would have asked themselves what was this team doing in the Second Division in the first place.

But the 32-year old West Ham skipper had reasons to be confident. Bonds was a highly experienced player and captain of the victorious 1975 Cup-winning side. More or less recovered from his long-standing injury problems, Bonds was fit for the Final and raring to go. But despite the skipper's belief in his team, the North London side were everybody's clear favourites on the day.

Hammers fans arriving at the stadium without a ticket would not have had a problem because they could find a friendly tout willing to part with a ticket at the Hammers end for a very reasonable £30. They could then join the supporters of both teams heading up Wembley Way, full of expectation. The area around the entrance to the stadium was a sea of claret and blue, and the noise from those already safely inside the ground added to the mounting excitement.

The build-up to the game passed in a flash before the teams, both in their normal colours, were led onto the field by their respective managers, John Lyall and Terry Neil. Before the kick-off the two captains, Bonds and Pat Rice, presented their teams to the Duke and Duchess of Kent, while 'I'm forever blowing bubbles' rang round the ground, drowning all attempts by the Arsenal fans to make themselves heard. At that moment, seconds before 3 o'clock, the atmosphere in the ground was electric.

Then something odd happened. A portly figure wandered onto the pitch, carrying half a dozen cameras round his neck, and took his place just to the right of the goal at the West Ham end. To the utter confusion of the opposition fans, Hammers faithful began chanting at the top of their voices, 'There is only one Stevie Bacon, one Stevie Bacon.' The fans were paying their own tribute to the Stratford Express's legendary cameraman, Steve Bacon, who was to become the club's official photographer. Bacon was loved and respected at Upton Park, and the fans' tribute was a genuine gesture of appreciation and gratitude by the fans to one of their own.

The game opened with Arsenal having the majority of possession, with Brady pulling most of the strings. But the Hammers had a plan and refused to grant the great Irishman the freedom of Wembley. John Lyall had gambled on choosing the young midfielder Paul Allen ahead of more experienced players. Lyall, a great tactician in the Greenwood mould, detailed Allen, the youngest player to appear in an FA Cup Final, aged 17 years and 256 days, to stick close to Brady and stop him

*Frank Lampard and Arsenal's Liam Brady take a tumble in the 1980 FA Cup Final at Wembley.*

*The goal that won the FA Cup. Trevor Brooking's low header which proved the only goal of the 1980 Final.*

dictating the play. The teenager and the tenacious Geoff Pike fought tirelessly to disrupt the usually smooth Arsenal passing game. By stifling the opposition's best players, these two unsung heroes gave the Hammer's more creative midfielders, Devonshire and Brooking, plenty of opportunities to counter-attack.

With Allen snapping at his heels Brady became less influential, and then a claret-and-blue miracle occurred. In the 12th minute, with the Hammers forced to play on the counter-attack, Devonshire broke free on the left wing and delivered a measured cross into the Gunners' penalty area. The ball fell to centre-forward David 'Psycho' Cross, whose half-hit shot was parried by Pat Jennings. The rebound fell neatly for Stuart Pearson, who scuffed his shot across the goalmouth. Waiting was the Hammers' England star, Trevor Brooking, who stooped and deflected the ball into the net with his head. The Gunners' celebrated defence was helpless.

Yes, Brooking had scored with a header in the Cup Final against Arsenal – a miracle indeed – and West Ham were 1–0 ahead. Needless to say, the Irons' fans went wild, and not for the last time that May afternoon Bubbles rang around Wembley. Brooking must have relished the moment. In the days before the match, Nottingham Forest manager Brian Clough singled out Brooking for criticism when he alleged the classy midfielder floated like a butterfly and stung like one. Clough accused the East London club of being more interested in the glamour of Wembley than in being promoted back to the top flight, not that it was any of old Big Mouth's business. Clough later apologised to Brooking for his scandalous remarks.

Having taken the lead, could the West End side retain it? The Gunners dominated the last 30 minutes of the first half, but the Hammers defence held firm, with Bonds, Martin and 'keeper Parkes outstanding. The best efforts of Sunderland, Stapleton and Rix foundered on the rock of the claret-and-blue defence. The East Londoners reached the interval unscathed.

During the interval the Hammers fans speculated nervously about what might happen in the second period. Over the year they had become hardened to disappointment, but from the evidence of the first 45 minutes they were entitled to believe that this time their dreams wouldn't fade and die.

The second half continued the pattern of the first, but with one encouraging exception. As Devonshire and Brooking grew in confidence, they started running at the Arsenal defence. The Hammers rearguard took heart in their teammates attacking intentions as they withstood everything the tireless Brady could throw at them. With minutes to go the claret-and-blue hordes began to prepare for victory. Their team almost scored a second goal, which would have put the 1980 Cup Final beyond doubt.

The young Allen skipped through the Gunners' defence, and with only Pat Jennings to beat he was cynically and cruelly brought down by an appalling Willie Young tackle. Young remained on the field and only received a yellow card – the professional foul rule had not yet been introduced. But justice was well and truly done when the referee blew for time minutes later and the jubilant Hammers fans could celebrate at last.

Billy Bonds received the FA Cup from the Duke of York. He turned to his left and lifted the trophy joyously to the victorious legions of West Ham fans below. For once the Hammers' fortunes failed to find a hiding place, and the East End was about to enjoy its momentary place in the sun.

In truth, the game itself was a pretty dull affair for the uncommitted – FA Cup Finals often turn out this way, with both sets of players inhibited by nerves and fear of failure. But such a negative thought never crossed the fans' minds as they made their way back down Wembley Way. As they approached the subway leading to the underground station, a spontaneous outburst of singing broke out, which continued onto the station platform and on the trains heading east. One by one supporters sang their tribute to the West Ham legends of the past, with pride of place given to the saintly Bobby Moore.

The next day the sun continued to shine for the victory procession, which began in Stratford Broadway, just across the road from Bobby Moore's own pub, Mooro's. The police estimated that over 200,000 people lined the East End streets to show their appreciation and join in the fun. The team's open-top bus took over two hours to cover the short journey to its destination, East Ham Town Hall. Trevor Brooking expressed his own feelings about the team's reception that Sunday: 'The old East End did know how to celebrate and people came out of hospitals and babies were held up crying their eyes out. The atmosphere was fantastic on that Sunday because winning a match like that against Arsenal was something that the East End wanted to celebrate. It is something I will always remember.'

Billy Bonds later said he couldn't remember much about the celebrations apart from putting the club coach, Ernie Gregory, and physio, Rob Jenkins, to bed early because they had both drunk too much champagne – straight out of the FA Cup itself – and why not?

With typical generosity, Bonds attributed the victory to his manager, John Lyall: 'John got his tactics spot on. He brought Stuart Pearson back into midfield and left David Cross up front and played five across the middle with Geoff Pike chasing everything down.' Brooking echoed his captain's tribute, recognising the manager's tactical brain: 'John said that the game plan was that we get the ball and then pass it well. West Ham sides have always been brought up to pass the ball, and John had taken up Ron Greenwood's mantle and had the same coaching philosophy, the one that got us back into the top level the following season.'

Billy Bonds, Trevor Brooking, Frank Lampard, Alan Devonshire, Alvin Martin and Phil Parkes were wonderful West Ham players who would be included in most fans' all-time West Ham XI. Geoff Pike, Ray Stewart and Paul Allen pushed them close. The 1980 side must be regarded as one of the best in the club's history, led by its most successful coach, John Lyall.

The 1980 Cup Final was the last major trophy won by the club. Since that glorious day the Hammers have been beset with problems on and off the pitch. The 1980s and 1990s brought a much-improved stadium but at the expense of massive debt, bond schemes, a squandering of the club's most outstanding young players for a generation, managerial incompetence and boardroom farces beyond the imagination of Brian Rix – you just couldn't make it up. Only the fans have remained constant in their loyalty and unwavering support. On that Saturday in May 1980 they thoroughly deserved their day in the sun.

**Final score: West Ham United 1 Arsenal 0**
West Ham United: Parkes, Stewart, Lampard, Bonds, Martin, Devonshire, Allen, Pearson, Cross, Brooking, Pike.
Substitutes: Brush.

# 18.

# WEST HAM UNITED
# V LIVERPOOL

## LEAGUE CUP FINAL                    14 MARCH 1981

On 14 March 1981 West Ham were 10 points clear at the top of the Second Division and heading back to the top flight of English football. John Lyall's men were enjoying a wonderful season. Less than a year after defeating Arsenal in the 1980 FA Cup Final, they were back at Wembley, this time in the Final of the Football League Cup. A formidable Liverpool side provided the opposition, and the Hammers were again cast as firm underdogs. The West Ham players would have relished the thought of a second Everest-like challenge against, arguably, the best side in the Europe.

The Hammers' Wembley opponents were English and European Champions, and if the Merseyside team needed motivation the League Cup remained the only trophy the club had never won. The Liverpool side for the Final included such famous Anfield names as Kenny Dalglish, Alan Hansen, Graeme Souness, Ray Kennedy, Sammy Lee and Terry McDermott. They had a substitute that day in Jimmy Case, who would have walked into any other First Division side. They were only missing Ian Rush, who returned for the replay at Villa Park.

The two teams had faced each other at the start of the 1980–81 season, Liverpool beating the Hammers 1–0 in the Charity Shield, with the winning goal scored by Terry McDermott. But by the end of the

*League Cup Final ticket.*

*League Cup Final programme.*

season the Hammers were brimming with confidence, having beaten First Division opponents in Tottenham and Coventry on their way to the Final.

The Hammers' side at Wembley was more or less the same as the one against Arsenal in the 1980 FA Cup Final. Jimmy Neighbour came in for Paul Allen, while Paul Goddard replaced Stuart Pearson, who dropped to the bench. John Lyall had picked a very attacking side, and they were confident they could test the famous Anfield defence. It was a sparkling West Ham line up that today's supporters can only dream about, with ten Englishmen and one Scot, Stewart, making up the team. The match was refereed by Clive Thomas, a Welshman, who managed to upset the Hammers' players, management and fans with his controversial handling of the game.

A crowd of 100,000 packed into the old stadium to witness the North versus South clash. As this was the Football League Cup, tickets were evenly distributed between both sets of fans, which meant that, for once, Wembley was full of true football supporters. It was a real people's Final.

The pitch was wet and slippery from the start, encouraging both teams to fly into tackles, which resulted in a scrappy first half. The more creative players like Devonshire, Brooking and Dalglish were denied any time on the ball as the defences dominated the game.

Sammy Lee's early shot was ruled offside, and Parkes saved comfortably from Dalglish. At the other end the Hammers had little opportunity to stretch the Liverpool defence, although in a rare attack Goddard struck his volley just over Clemence's cross-bar. Alan Kennedy was lucky to stay on the pitch after a nasty foul on winger Neighbour, but the Hammers refused to intimidated and slowly began to

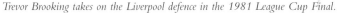

*Trevor Brooking takes on the Liverpool defence in the 1981 League Cup Final.*

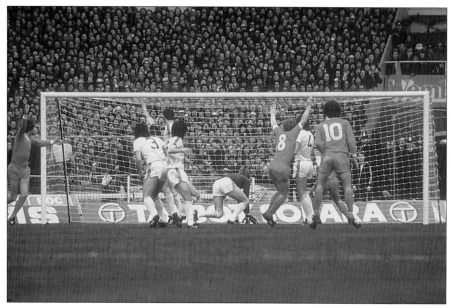

*Sammy Lee (8) is happy after Kennedy scores for Liverpool in the 1981 League Cup Final.*

find their feet as Brooking, Devonshire and Pike took control of midfield. Just on half-time Frank Lampard Snr joined the attack and thumped one of his typical efforts just past Clemence's far post. The England 'keeper was making his 32nd appearance at Wembley, and his experience was proving vital to his side.

The interval was reached in stalemate, each team cancelling out the other. But the Hammers were still very much in the game and could look forward to the second half with real belief.

To be brutally honest, the second half produced little of note apart from a few more crunching tackles. On one occasion Goddard broke free from Hansen, but Clemence was out quickly to smother the shot. Right on 90 minutes Billy Bonds stormed forward, only to direct his header wide of the Reds' goal. Bonds later admitted that the first 90 minutes produced very little to get the fans excited: 'All that really mattered came in the last few seconds of extra-time.'

Perhaps the players sensed the tense atmosphere in the ground. The capacity crowd were expecting more from so many great players, but the defences remained on top throughout. Surprisingly, on such a big pitch, the likes of Dalglish, Devonshire and Brooking had no room to produce the kind of football the crowd were expecting, and the result was a war of attrition. But for West Ham, a win remained a real possibility.

The game came alive in extra time. Alan Devonshire just failed to convert a Neighbour cross before Case, on for the tiring Heighway, smashed a drive against the bar. A few minutes later and, for the first time in the match, Cross found some space, but his header was acrobatically tipped over the bar by Clemence. Much to the displeasure of the Irons' supporters, Stuart Pearson was brought on for Goddard for the final 15 minutes, presumably to tighten up the midfield. With just three minutes left on the clock, the game suddenly exploded into life in the worst possible way for the Londoners.

Alan Kennedy thundered a 20-yard shot into the West Ham wall, laying out Sammy Lee in the process. The Hammers raced out in a unit as they had done a thousand times on the training ground. Kennedy smacked the rebound into the net over Lee, lying prostrate by the penalty spot. Parkes was helpless to intervene. The Hammers' well-drilled defence were relieved when the linesman raised his flag for offside, but to the astonishment of everyone in the ground, including the Liverpool supporters, Thomas overruled his linesman and allowed the goal to stand. The Cockney element of the crowd joined their manager in vehement protest, but the Hammers, for all their protests, were 1–0 down and heading for defeat.

The tension on the pitch threatened to overspill into violence, with Stewart gaining revenge on Kennedy for his first-half challenge on young Neighbour. The full-back chased Kennedy half the length of the field but referee Thomas let Stewart off with a caution. 100,000 people knew why. West Ham poured forward in a desperate effort to equalise, Devonshire tricking his way past two Liverpool defenders before being cynically fouled. The furious Stewart hammered the free-kick at Clemence, who showed his class and calmly tipped the ball over the bar. With their supporters urging them forward, the Londoners were doing everything they could to get back into the game.

The Hammers were not to be denied. Jimmy Neighbour drove the resultant corner high into the Liverpool penalty area and onto the head of Alvin 'Stretch' Martin, who powered the ball past the helpless Clemence. As the Hammers supporters rose to their feet in anticipation of a goal, McDermott, standing on the line, deflected the ball over the bar with his hand. It was no goal but a nailed-on penalty.

You could have heard a pin drop in the ground as regular penalty-taker Stewart stepped up to take the kick. The Hammers fans were confident that their man would score – the Scot rarely missed a penalty. After a quick, reassuring word from skipper Bonds, Stewart ran up, with 100,000 people holding their breath, and coolly placed a precise kick past Clemence for the equaliser. Stewart later recalled, 'I knew the pressure was on. And the ball seemed to bounce 15,000 times before it reached the net, but I knew it was in from the moment it left my foot. It was a dream come true.'

The match was over, but not before John Lyall was booked after an angry spat with the referee. The West Ham manager was still furious with the Welshman for allowing Kennedy's goal. But nothing could spoil the day for the Hammers supporters. The after-match formalities were a little bizarre as both teams climbed up to the Royal Box to receive their medals before embarking on the traditional lap of honour.

For the Irons justice was done. It was gratifying that Jimmy Neighbour played his part in the equalising goal. Jimmy was a local lad, and although he played for Tottenham early in his career, the West Ham supporters claimed him for themselves. West Ham paid £150,000 for the winger, and he was an immediate hit with the fans. Jimbo scored the winner in the semi-final against Cardiff in 1981 to put his side back at Wembley, and Billy Bonds knew his value to the team. He said of the winger, 'Little Jimbo was always among the most popular men among teammates.' Neighbour later joined Bournemouth on a loan spell, and he played for a short time in America before retiring as a player. The winger returned to Upton Park as Youth-team trainer and coached at Enfield Town when the club won the FA Trophy in 1988. To the delight of local youngsters and their dads, he opened a sports shop in Station Road, Chingford, close to his family and friends. Jimmy Neighbour died tragically of a heart attack at his home in Woodford on 11 April 2009, aged 58. He is sorely missed by everyone who knew him.

The much-anticipated replay was held at Villa Park on 1 April. Liverpool brought back Phil Thompson for Irwin and Ian Rush for Heighway, while Jimmy Case replaced the injured Graham Souness. These changes probably strengthened rather than weakened the Merseysiders. The Hammers were unchanged.

Despite his problems in the first match, Clive Thomas was again the referee. This did not trouble the Hammers' skipper. Bonds said at the time, 'I considered him a good ref, largely because you knew where you were with him.'

He agreed that Thomas had made a mistake at Wembley, but Bonds was a good-enough professional to know his team needed to put the controversy behind them. They certainly started the match with a positive attitude and no thought of refereeing issues.

Paul Goddard gave the travelling supporters hope by giving his team an early lead with a well-taken header. But on this occasion Liverpool were too strong for the East Londoners and won comfortably with goals by Alan Hansen and Kenny Dalglish. It was no disgrace for the Hammers to lose an FA Cup Rinal replay to the English and European champions, and they had the consolation of winning promotion back to the top flight of English football.

Paul Goddard, the Hammers' goalscorer in the replay was nicknamed 'Sarge' by his teammates because of his involvement with the Scouts and his obvious leadership qualities. West Ham paid Queen's Park Rangers £800,000 for Goddard in 1980. He made 213 appearances and scored 71 goals, a good return for a player who was popular at Upton Park. Goddard notched 5 goals for the England Under-23 side and scored in his only full international against Iceland in 1982. He left the Hammers for Newcastle United but returned briefly as assistant manager, leaving just after Alan Pardew joined the club.

In truth, Goddard's goal hardly mattered. Despite their Wembley heroics the Hammers were well-beaten on the night. Professional footballers hate losing Cup Finals, and some of the side had experienced defeat at the hands of Frankfurt in the

European Cup-Winners' Cup Final. As Billy Bonds said, 'All you can do is try and show dignity in defeat – while the winners are rushing about celebrating.'

John Lyall escaped punishment for his outburst against Clive Thomas when he was later exonerated by the FA. The manager had a busy summer ahead, preparing his team for their forthcoming season in Division One. Despite the defeat against Liverpool, West Ham could look forward to the next few seasons with growing confidence. They won the Second Division Championship in 1981, had reached the Final of the Football League Cup and the last eight of the Cup-Winners' Cup and had their best group of players for some years.

**Final score: West Ham United 1 Liverpool 1**

West Ham United: Parkes, Stewart, Lampard, Bonds (captain), Martin, Devonshire, Neighbour, Goddard, Cross, Brooking, Pike, Pearson.

# 19.

# WEST HAM UNITED
# V BURY TOWN

## THE MILK CUP
## SECOND ROUND                    25 OCTOBER 1983

The Hammers stepped up their game on their return to the First Division in 1981, finishing ninth and eighth in their first two years back in the top flight. The Greenwood/Lyall dynasty clearly had a few years to run, despite the disappointment of the odd season in the Second Division.

The young Paul Allen began to establish himself in the side, and the manager brought in Steve Walford and Dave Swindlehurst to add a bit of experience and as counter-weights to the silky skills of Brooking, Devonshire and the emerging Tony Cottee.

On the night of the 25 October 1983 Cottee signalled his arrival in the top flight with four goals in West Ham's record 10–0 in the second round second-leg match against Bury Town. The Hammers won the first leg 2–1 and most of the fans thought the return game would be a formality. As a result just 10,896 people turned up at Upton Park that night to witness the goal feast. It was the club's lowest gate in 30 years.

Anthony 'Tony' Cottee was born in Plaistow, just down the road from the Boleyn. He established his place in the first team in the 1983–84 season aged only 18, and he scored 15 League goals. In the following season he did even better with 17, enhancing his growing reputation in the process. By the age of 20 Cottee had scored an impressive 37 League goals for the club.

The budding centre-forward was voted PFA Young Player of the Year in 1986, and his goals helped West Ham to reach their highest-ever League position. The club finished third that season and were a frustrating four points away from the League title. That season Cottee began his prolific partnership with the Scot, Frank

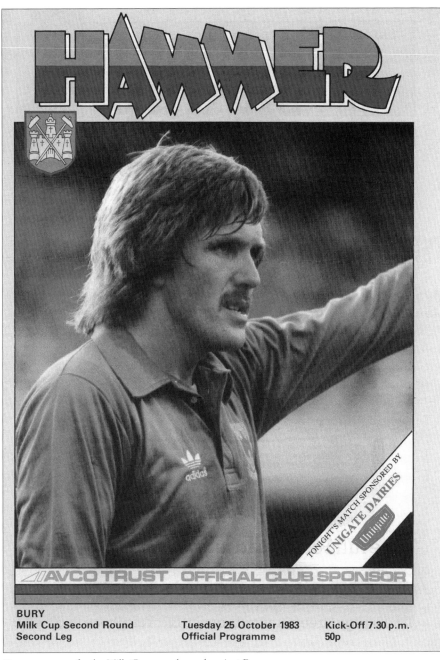

**BURY**
Milk Cup Second Round
Second Leg

Tuesday 25 October 1983
Official Programme

Kick-Off 7.30 p.m.
50p

*Programme cover for the Milk Cup second round against Bury.*

McAvennie, and the pair scored 46 goals between them, Cottee contributing 20 and McAvennie 26. The diminutive dynamo scored 93 League goals in 212 games from 1982 to 1988 and became a true West Ham legend. Inevitably, he was sold after McAvennie returned to Scotland and Lyall's men began to struggle in the League. Once again, West Ham had managed to mishandle two of its greatest talents. Once the pair had left Upton Park the team began to slide down the table.

Cottee scored a hat-trick for Everton on his debut, but the Merseysiders failed to win a trophy while he was at the club, although they did reach the FA Cup Final. He returned in 1994 for his second spell at Upton Park and continued to score important goals for his beloved Irons. Towards the end of his distinguished career Cottee spent a couple of years at Leicester City, and at the age of 35 he helped his new club win the Football League Cup – the only trophy of his long career. The supremely talented Plaistow boy gained seven England caps between 1986 and 1989 but failed to score a single goal for his country. Cottee remains a passionate West Ham supporter and can often be seen at the ground in his role as a highly-regarded TV commentator.

Goalkeeper Phil Parkes appeared on the front cover of the programme on the evening of the Bury match, but he could easily have been at home with his feet up – nobody would have noticed. The first goal came in the second minute, when Steve Walford's cross was nodded on by Swindlehurst and Cottee slid in from close range. The tie was over from this point, but Cottee and the home crowd were hungry for goals, and they came in buckets.

At 1–0 on the night, Bury were offered a lifeline when they were awarded a penalty after a Bonds foul. John Bramhall stepped up to take the kick and hammered his shot against a post. This was not going to be Bury's night.

Cottee's first-half hat-trick ensured the home side went in for the interval with an unassailable 5–0 lead. Alvin Martin joined in the fun, heading in Stewart's cross in the 18th minute, but the goal of the half was scored by Trevor Brooking. The England midfielder was at his sumptuous best and at the heart of every attacking move. Midway through the first half he set off on a 40-yard run, waltzing through half the Bury defence before hitting a precise shot into the top corner.

John Lyall withdrew Billy Bonds at half-time to keep him out of trouble with referee David Letts, who, for some reason, was winding up the skipper that night. But his team were in no mood to show mercy as they kept up the pressure on their humiliated opponents. Cottee quickly claimed his fourth, slamming home Martin's deflected header from a Devonshire cross. The Hammers' attack was running riot. On 65 minutes Devonshire picked up the ball in his own half and ghosted through the Shakers' defence to make it seven. A couple of minutes later the midfielder was pulled down in the penalty area following another mazy run. Reliable penalty-taker Stewart drove the spot-kick high into the net to make it eight.

Not content with eight, the Hammers, urged on by the crowd, wanted double figures. The Bury defence was powerless to stop Devonshire and Brooking in such an irresistible mood. The record ninth was scored by Brooking, whose deflected shot looped over the Bury 'keeper and into the net. The pair linked up again a few minutes later. Devonshire drove forward before releasing the ball to his midfield partner, who had the simple task of the tapping the ball into the net for his side's 10th goal of the night. What a memorable match for the few thousand supporters at the Boleyn that night as they crushed their lower division opponents.

Winning 10–0, even against Bury Town, has to be a special and memorable occasion, certainly for West Ham fans. But more than anything the match highlighted the importance of two players – Tony Cottee and the incomparable Alan Devonshire. The midfielder was adored at Upton Park and was everything the fans wanted from their players. He was a joy to watch, with his delightful skills, football intelligence, and commitment to the club. Devonshire operated on the left of midfield and linked brilliantly with Brooking, who played more centrally. Geoff Pike uncomplainingly did the donkey work for his two colleagues.

The dance record label On-U Sound recorded a tribute to their favourite Hammer titled Alan Alan Devonshire, a chant that tumbled down the North Bank every time the stylish number 10 went on one of his mazy runs. Devonshire must rank alongside Moore, Hurst, Peters, Bonds and Brooking himself as one of the West Ham post-war greats. He played his debut match in 1976 against West Brom and made 358 appearances for the Hammers in his 14 years at the club. Though not a prolific goalscorer – a modest 30 goals in his career – his assist record must have been phenomenal. One of the most creative players of his generation, there were nights when Devonshire's breathtaking displays lit up the night sky at Upton Park.

Devonshire played just eight times for England between 1980 and 1983, but he probably should have won 50 caps. His life was steeped in football – his dad was a professional with Chester City and Crystal Palace – and it was no surprise to anyone when he took up coaching at the end of his playing days. He is currently the successful manager of Hampton & Richmond FC, who, under his leadership, won promotion to the Conference at the end of the 2009–10 season. Alan Devonshire must be one of the few players to have a racehorse named after him. His contribution to the Hammers' side of the 1980s will remain long in the memory.

An interesting story about the 10–0 win over Bury is that it was captured on film by a young cameraman called Steve Katz. Thanks to him, West Ham's record win is preserved for posterity. His film should be shown again and again to the team of 2010, just to remind them of their ancestry, although it might be regarded as a horror show in Bury.

**Final score: West Ham United 10 Bury Town 0**
West Ham United: Parkes, Stewart, Gallagher, Dickens, Martin, Devonshire, Van der Elst, Cottee, Clark, Allen, Pike, Morgan.

# 20.

# WEST HAM UNITED

# V NEWCASTLE UNITED

## DIVISION ONE                    21 APRIL 1986

A list of West Ham's most memorable matches must include at least one from 1985–86. They finished their Division One season in third place, the club's highest-ever League finish, with a colossal 84 points. Astonishingly, the Hammers had accumulated 40 of those points by Christmas. They were also safe from relegation with only half of the fixtures played.

There were a few stand-out games that season, including a 4–0 away win in a mud-bath against Chelsea, with two goals from Cottee and one apiece for McAvennie and Devonshire. There was an interesting end-of-season classic at home against Ipswich Town, which ended in a 2–2 draw. The match was a relegation battle for the Tractor Boys, while West Ham were challenging for second place. Earlier in the season the clubs had been involved in a marathon fourth-round FA Cup tie, which the Hammers eventually won after a second replay at snow-covered Portman Road.

In his years as manager John Lyall had made few changes to his side, but he began to realise he needed some new faces if the Hammers were going to mount a serious League challenge. Lyall brought in Neil Orr for the seriously injured Geoff Pike, Stewart Robson and the mercurial and combative Mark Ward. Tony Gale came in for Alvin Martin, while George Parris and Alan Dickens had emerged from the Academy as real contenders for the first team. Sadly, the transfer of the inspirational Liam Brady from Arsenal was not finalised until the following season.

George Parris and Alan Dickens both played in the Newcastle game and slotted straight into Hammers' passing game. Dickens was almost a Devonshire clone, if there could ever be such a thing. Nobody could compare with the master, but Dickens came close – he even looked like the great man. His easy first touch, smooth running and passing ability contrasted with Parris's more physical presence. The young full-back came in for some awful racial abuse in his first few seasons,

*Programme cover from the Newcastle game.*

particularly at Chelsea, but he was a strong character and it never affected his performance.

Both Alvin Martin and Tony Gale played against Newcastle and, like Dickens and Devonshire, were very similar players. Martin was brought to the club by Ron Greenwood in 1977 at the age of 14. The Bootle-born centre-half played over 600 games for the Hammers and is one of only two players to receive a second testimonial at Upton Park, the other being Billy Bonds. Martin's consistent performances for his club earned him 17 caps for England under Ron Greenwood and Bobby Robson.

Tony Gale was signed from Fulham and played for the Hammers between 1984 and 1995. He was a strong centre-half in the Martin mould, if not quite as effective as his defensive partner. Martin and Gale were good servants of the club, and both are still seen regularly at Upton Park. Gale writes a fans' blog and, like his old defensive partner, is a pundit for radio and TV.

There have been around 150 hat-tricks in the history of West Ham United, but centre-half trebles are an extremely rare commodity. This was one match Alvin Martin would remember for a very long time. As hat-tricks go, this was one was one of the most surreal, with each of Martin's three goals scored against a different goalkeeper. Martin said after the game, 'It's not often that a centre-half gets a hat-trick, and that was probably the worst one anybody has scored...But it's in the record books.'

The Hammers were riding high in the League in April, and Willie McFaul's Newcastle side were in 10th place following a draw at Stamford Bridge the previous Saturday. The home side were slight favourites for the match, but nobody was prepared for what happened that Monday night.

*Alan Devonshire evades a tackle by Glen Roeder in the Hammers' magnificent 8-1 victory over Newcastle United in April 1986, as West Ham strode on towards their best-ever finishing place in Division One.*

With goalkeeper McKellar carrying an injury, the Geordies began the game on the back-foot. In the fifth minute the deluge began when Martin volleyed home Devonshire's free-kick. Long-range efforts from Stewart and Orr both found the back of the net to make the score 3–0, before the future West Ham manager, Glen Roeder, guided the ball into his own net, much to the delight of almost all the 25,000 people in the ground. Later he said, 'It was the only way I could stop Cottee from scoring.'

The Geordie 'keeper failed to appear for the second half. He was suffering from either a shoulder injury or deep psychological damage, whichever you prefer. Chris Hedworth donned the green jersey and almost immediately tumbled awkwardly, cracking his collar bone as he fell, but not before Martin collected his second, heading in Gale's flick on from Ward's corner.

To the great surprise and amusement of the North Bank, Newcastle's third 'keeper of the night was none other than England international, the diminutive Peter Beardsley. Almost immediately Billy Whitehurst scored a consolation goal for the visitors, but Beardsley was share the same fate as his predecessors in the Newcastle goal as first substitute Goddard then McAvennie notched to make it 7–1.

Great drama followed when the Hammers were awarded a penalty with six minutes to go. Ray Stewart was the usual penalty-taker, and he was one of the very best. But, with the crowd singing his name, Alvin Martin stepped forward and casually stroked the ball past his England colleague to seal his rather bizarre hat-trick. In the last few minutes the walking-wounded Geordies fought hard to keep the score under double figures.

To win 8–0 against Newcastle in the old Division One has to be a towering performance by any standards. For your centre-half to score a hat-trick is surely an indication of the attacking instincts of the players. This match had everything for Hammers supporters, – goals and sumptuous football from Devonshire, Ward and Cottee. In addition there was the hilarious sight of the opposition field three different 'keepers, each of whom conceded a goal – ideal material for a football quiz question. Add to that the future West Ham manager putting through his own net while part of a defence that let in eight goals, and that was the lot. All fans really needed that Monday night at Upton Park was a goal from Tony Cottee, but unbelievably the Hammers' goal machine failed to score in this very strange match.

Finishing third behind Everton and Liverpool was a fine achievement for the Hammers that season, but it was nearly so much better. They went into the final Saturday of the season with a realistic chance of winning the First Division for the first time in their history, but the supporters' dreams were shattered by Liverpool's victory at Chelsea on that last day.

**Final score: West Ham United 8 Newcastle United 1**
West Ham United: Parkes, Stewart, Parris, Gale, Martin, Devonshire, Ward, McAvennie, Dickens, Cottee, Goddard.
Substitutes: Orr.

# 21.

# WEST HAM UNITED

# V NOTTINGHAM FOREST

## DIVISION ONE                    21 NOVEMBER 1988

The wonderful season of 1985–86 turned out to be a false dawn for the Hammers as they failed to build on their highest-ever League finish. Life became very difficult for John Lyall as the club lost its way on and off the pitch. Within three years the inevitable happened, and Lyall was unceremoniously sacked.

The supporters were relishing the thought of a few years at the top, with the coveted Division One title a real prospect. But the 1986–87 season, instead of heralding a new era, brought bitter disappointment and frustration. The downturn in the Hammers' fortunes illustrates perfectly the club's ability to bounce between near perfection and total humiliation in the space of a few short years. It is simply the destiny of West Ham United.

There was little of note to celebrate from Upton Park in the late 1980s, apart from one or two memorable moments, including the last few games of that great servant of the club, the one and only Billy Bonds. Like Moore before him, it was difficult to imagine the Hammers without their swashbuckling hero. There were also a couple of games where the old embers burst into temporary flame only to fizzle out to nothing.

One of the few highlights of 1986–87 was a thumping 5–3 win over Chelsea and, towards the end of the season, a satisfying 3–1 defeat of Arsenal at Upton Park. The latter saw the great Liam Brady, who played 11 games for the Hammers in his debut season, playing against his former club. Brady, after taking some fierce stick from the Gooners in the ground, scored the winning goal for the Hammers, much to the delight of the home fans. Brady's celebrations, which involved running the length of the Chicken Run, were regarded as excessive by the referee, who immediately booked the Irishman. As Hammers' historian Martin Godleman has written, it was a seminal moment of the great Irishman's short career at Upton Park. Seven years

*Programme cover from the Division One game against Nottingham Forest.*

previously the midfielder had been doing his brilliant best to beat his new club at Wembley in the 1980 Cup Final. Also playing that day was former Gunner Stewart Robson, the West Ham captain.

The year was notable for the continued goalscoring exploits of Tony Cottee, who scored twice against Arsenal and ended the season with a higher goal tally than in the previous season, when the Hammers had finished third. This was a significant achievement because Cottee was without his goalscoring accomplice for much of the campaign, the one-season wonder Scot, Frank McAvennie.

In the late 1980s the fans witnessed the beginning of the end of the Lyall era at Upton Park, and they didn't like what they saw. McAvennie left early in the 1986–87 season, and even the goals from the ever-reliable Cottee began to dry up. In 1987–88 the increasingly frustrated fans enjoyed just six wins in 20 home matches as the Hammers languished at the lower end of the table.

One of the home wins that season was memorable for a number of reasons, firstly for being a rare home victory; secondly for Tony Cottee's two goals; and finally for one last rousing performance at the Boleyn by the veteran Billy Bonds. But the most memorable reason was that this match marked a sharp decline in the Hammer's fortunes, while at the same time it showed just what they could have achieved with a little more application and strong leadership at all levels of the club.

Forest were riding high in the top half of the table when they arrived at Upton Park. They had players of the calibre of Nigel Clough and Neil Webb, and the home fans must have made their weary way to the ground more in hope than expectation. But, despite their depressing form, the Hammers had some decent players of their own. Apart from Bonds and Cottee, the team included Ray Stewart, Alan Dickens, Kevin Keen and 19-year-old wonder-boy Paul Ince.

In front of a disappointing 17,000 fans, the Hammers started the game strongly, and their attacking instincts paid off in the 14th minute when Cottee scored with a looping header from a Keen cross. Keen was running riot on the wing, and his crosses were proving difficult for the Forest defence to handle. Keen was a wonderful player; skilful and quick, he seemed to glide over the pitch and formed an excellent partnership with Mark Ward. For a time, like Alan Dickens, Keen briefly threatened to be the new Brooking or Devonshire, but instead he made his mark as a coach at Upton Park.

Halfway through the first half of an entertaining game, England international Neil Webb played a neat one-two with Wilkinson before firing a shot into the top corner to put his team back on level terms. The half ended with the Hammers well on top and dominating midfield through the young Ince, Dickens, Ward and Keen.

A twice-taken Stewart penalty put the Hammers back in the lead in the 52nd minute, and just two minutes later came the goal of the match. For the umpteenth time Ward broke down the right and knocked a deep cross over the Forest defence. Tony Cottee dropped off his marker, found space and his spectacular scissor-kick flew into the net. The home supporters were dancing on the terraces in celebration

– they had little else to cheer about that season. Cottee has since described his goal against Forest as 'the greatest of my career'.

Young Nigel Clough, perhaps out to impress his dad, scored a late consolation goal for his side. Brian Clough's Forest never knew when they were beaten, but despite their best efforts they failed to penetrate the stubborn Hammers' defence, and the Londoners secured a vital win.

In truth the memorable win over Forest was a mere flash in the pan, and the Hammers finished the season in 16th place, 33 points behind Forest and miles behind champions Everton. However, despite Cottee leaving after six years and 118 goals, there were some signs of encouragement for the Upton Park faithful: Paul Ince was beginning to realise his immense potential, Julian Dicks was signed from Bristol and the mercurial Stuart Slater stepped up from the youth team. Ince, Dicks and Slater, along with Dickens, Keen and Ward, should have formed the core of a trophy-chasing side at Upton Park, but sadly it never happened. This constant squandering of young talent is a recent development at the club and would never have happened under Malcolm Allison, Noel Cantwell and Ron Greenwood.

There was an interesting event during a West Ham versus Forest match from the previous season, which involved Billy Bonds. The match took place just after Bonds was awarded his MBE, and the Forest chairman, Maurice Roworth presented Bonds with a magnificent cut-glass vase in recognition of his honour on behalf of his club. The chairman had assumed this would be the veteran full-back's final appearance against Forest, and while presenting the gift, Roworth said, 'I don't suppose we'll be seeing you here again, Billy.' Little did he know that Billy Bonds MBE would play in this 3–2 defeat of Forest at Upton Park the following season, a game Bonds admitted was the Hammers' best performance of a disappointing campaign. This time there was no presentation, but Bonds was touched by the Forest chairman's generous gesture at the City Ground.

The match against Forest in November 1988 was memorable for a famous victory and a fabulous goal, but it turned out to be a jewel in a very rusty crown.

**Final score: West Ham United 3 Nottingham Forest 2**
West Ham United: McKnight, Bonds, Parris, Hilton, Stewart, Keen, Ward, Dickens, Ince, Cottee, Robson.

# 22.

# WEST HAM UNITED V LIVERPOOL

## LITTLEWOODS CUP
## FOURTH ROUND                    30 NOVEMBER 1988

The Premier League was still four years away in 1988, but the Boleyn was gradually being improved, with the Chicken Run replaced by a modern, if characterless, stand. Season tickets were available for most parts of the ground, but we had not yet reached the stage of luxury hotels, all-seater stadia and extravagant boxes.

At the end of November that season, the top flight had a rather bizarre look. Norwich City were top of Division One ahead of Arsenal, Liverpool and Millwall. The Hammers were second from bottom, just in front of Newcastle. Bobby Robson's England squad for the 1988 European Championships in Germany did not include a single West Ham player, and the brilliant Holland team exposed all of England's usual frailties on their way to taking the title.

Elsewhere in sport, Ben Johnson took the 100m gold medal in the 1988 Olympics in Seoul, only to be disqualified for taking performance-enhancing drugs. Mark Spitz didn't need any external stimulus in winning seven swimming gold medals. The Hammers could never be accused of taking stimulants as they staggered through the season – they had only escaped relegation the previous season by a whisker. The one consolation for the fans that year was a semi-final place in the Football League Cup.

League champions Liverpool arrived at Upton Park in November expecting a relatively easy victory on their way to yet another trophy, but Kenny Dalglish's side returned home with their tails firmly between their legs after experiencing their heaviest Cup defeat in the post-war period. They came up against a West Ham side

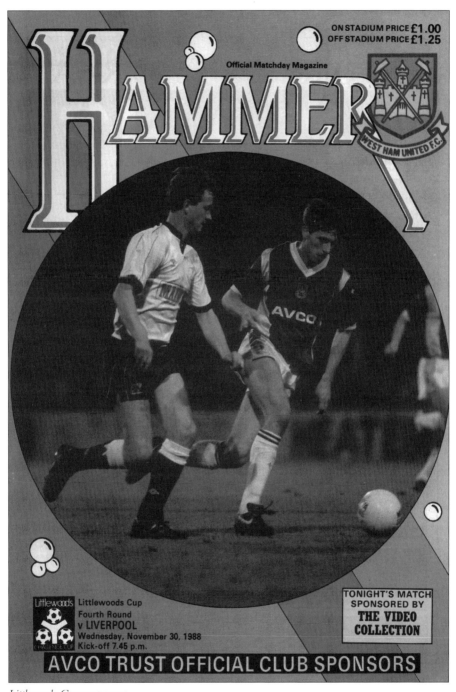

*Littlewoods Cup programme.*

*Home ticket for the fourth round home Littlewoods Cup match.*

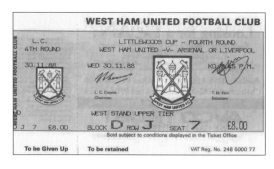

in unbelievable form on the night. The match proved to be one of a number of important games between the two clubs in the subsequent years.

John Lyall's side looked strong that season, as it did most years. Brady and Devonshire were approaching the veteran stage but remained hugely effective players. Steve Potts, Julian Dicks and Alan Dickens could play and run all day, and with David Kelly and Leroy Rosenior up front there should have been no shortage of goals.

Playing in the Hammers' midfield against Liverpool was one of the most controversial youngsters ever to represent the club. Paul Ince enjoyed his greatest game for West Ham that evening, and everyone at Upton Park assumed he was the future of the club – the new Moore and Brooking rolled into one. Six months later he became the most hated figure in the club's history when he was photographed wearing a Manchester United shirt while still a West Ham player.

On the previous Saturday the Hammers had lost at home to Everton, and Lyall must have feared the worst against the likes of Beardsley, Nichol, Whelan and Aldridge. Whatever the manager said in his pre-match team-talk worked, though. The team produced a display of sensational football that came out of nowhere. At the heart of the vintage performance were the mature midfielders Devonshire and Brady.

'We had Brady and Devonshire playing together for the first time that season,' Lyall later revealed in his autobiography, *Just Like my Dreams*. 'I played Dev wide on the right for the first time in nine years – he was magnificent – and those two old heads helped the youngsters secure one of the most memorable Cup victories in my time at West Ham.'

Although Devonshire and Brady played brilliantly that night, it was the 21-year-old Ince who was at the heart of his team's sparkling show. Midway through the first half, the youngster twisted in mid-air and sent a spectacular volley soaring past Hooper in the Liverpool goal. With the Hammers ahead and at their brilliant best, Ince repeated the feat when he headed in Devonshire's 28th minute corner, sending most of the 28,000 crowd into dreamland.

Liverpool sides are nothing if not resilient, and somehow they crawled their way back into the game. They were awarded a penalty in the 32nd minute, when Alvin Martin bowled over John Aldridge in the box. The centre-forward picked himself up and calmly slid his spot-kick past McKnight. The goal took some of the shine out of the Hammers' first-half display, but their performance gave them real hope for the second half.

The home supporters and the West Ham team knew Liverpool would come out fighting in the second half – surely the Hammers could not repeat their dazzling first-half display. But the Hammers quickly showed they were in no mood to surrender to the champions, and on the hour the Reds' defence pressed the self-destruct button. After a breathtaking interchange on the right between Brady and Devonshire, Kelly knocked in a low cross, which Steve Staunton, in true comic style, turned into his own net, much to the delight of the celebrating home fans.

With their lead restored to two goals and urged on by the North Bank, the Hammers continued to drive forward. They were soon rewarded for their enterprising football when, in the 58th minute, the marauding Dicks was fouled on the edge of the penalty area. Tony Gale stepped up and curled a classy free-kick over the Red's defensive wall and into the top corner of the net. The Liverpool players trudged off at the end well beaten by a side that produced an exhibition of attacking football not seen at the Boleyn for a very long time.

The following day The Times praised the Hammers' thrilling performance: 'For half an hour, Liverpool could not withstand the West Ham force. They were as powerful as a tropical whirlwind.'

Kenny Dalglish admitted his side deserved nothing from the game. However, his opposite manager, John Lyall, was delighted with his team: 'It was a magical performance – a special night... I think we saw the emergence of a new young star.' Ince scored twice against the champions, refused a TV interview and went home quietly.

Paul Ince's life changed forever that night. Things may have been different if the Hammers had won the Football League Cup that year. Although they defeated Aston Villa in the quarter-finals, they lost to eventual runners-up Luton Town in the last four. The club's League form deteriorated further and they were relegated at the end of the season, finishing a miserable 19th out of 20 clubs. The fans suffered another season when their team grossly underachieved, but they could always remember the glorious night of the 30 November and imagine what might have been.

Relegation was the end for John Lyall. Following Greenwood's elevation to director of football at West Ham in 1974, Lyall was appointed manager. In his 708 games in charge at the club, he won two FA Cups, the Second Division Championship, took the club to their highest top-flight League position and acquired two players of the very highest quality in Phil Parkes and Ray Stewart. Lyall was extremely popular at Upton Park, and he had an excellent run by West Ham standards.

Lyall introduced a steely character to the team that was lacking in the Greenwood era, and at the same time he refused to ditch the club's proud tradition of attacking football. He was as claret and blue as it is possible to be, and the Upton Park faithful idolised him. Lyall had begun his career as a left-back and played for England Youth, but a serious knee injury forced him to give up playing at the 23. As a young professional he coached in schools in the afternoon, and when his injury ruined his playing career he willingly joined the club's coaching staff.

Club chairman Len Cearns summoned Lyall to his luxurious Chigwell villa and brutally sacked the club's most successful manager on the spot. The fans were horrified – West Ham, a family club, just did not behave like this. The club issued a terse 70-word statement announcing they had sacked Lyall after 34 years at the club as player, coach and manager.

The Ilford-born Lyall was given a testimonial by the club in 1964 that raised nearly £4,000, a decent sum at the time. He enjoyed a few successful years at Ipswich before retiring to his farm in his beloved Suffolk countryside. He died suddenly of a heart attack at the family home in April 2006. His leaving left a hole at the heart and soul of the club that has never been filled. The club staged a minute's silence at the next home game, but the fans, in tribute to his memory, sang 'John Lyall's claret-and-blue army' throughout the 60 seconds.

The Guardian's Julie Welch wrote this moving tribute: 'The former West Ham United and Ipswich Town manager John Lyall, who has died of a heart attack aged 66, was an affable man, an almost complete contrast to the brooding, preening, haunted characters in charge of teams today. His death comes two months after that of his mentor Ron Greenwood (obituary, February 10), whom he succeeded as manager in 1974.'

West Ham fans will always remember John Lyall for his integrity, leadership and tactical nous. The style of his side's 4–1 victory over Liverpool is his revered legacy, and that night was good as it gets at Upton Park.

**Final score: West Ham United 4 Liverpool 1**
West Ham United: McKnight, Potts, Dick, Gale, Martin, Devonshire, Brady, Dickens, Ince, Kelly, Rosenior.

# 23.

# WEST HAM UNITED

# V EVERTON

## FA CUP SIXTH ROUND          11 MARCH 1991

In the late 1980s and early 1990s West Ham bounced back and forwards between Division Two and the top flight. Billy Bonds' appointment as manager brought some much-needed stability to the club, and they enjoyed a few untroubled years in the new Premier League. But it was typical of the Hammers' fortunes that they were relegated the year before the glitzy new initiative radically transformed English football.

During this period the supporters had some encouraging Cup runs to balance the disappointment of relegation. The fans were both surprised and delighted when their team reached the semi-final of the FA Cup in 1991, while at the same time they were entering a battle with Oldham Athletic to decide who would end the season Second Division champions. The Hammers were drawn at home to Everton in the sixth round in the FA Cup, and the game against the Merseysiders was a memorable encounter for the supporters and for one player in particular.

The team owed their fans a good Cup run. The previous season they had suffered the humiliation of being knocked out in the third round by lowly Torquay United, and they had needed replays to see off Aldershot and Luton Town in the early rounds, with the Aldershot tie nearly ending in a typical West Ham Cup humiliation. They drew the first game at Upton Park but saved their fans further embarrassment when they hammered their plucky opponents 6–1 in the replay.

A routine home win against Wigan in the last 16 set up a plum quarter-final against Everton. The mood was bordering on the expectant when the Merseysiders arrived at the Boleyn early in March. West Ham hadn't won the FA Cup or any trophy since their victory against Arsenal in 1980. Why not this year?

The two teams ran out to a tremendous reception from the 30,000 in the ground, the largest crowd of the season at the Boleyn. The Irons' team was solid rather than spectacular, with no outstanding stars of the quality of Brooking, Devonshire or the

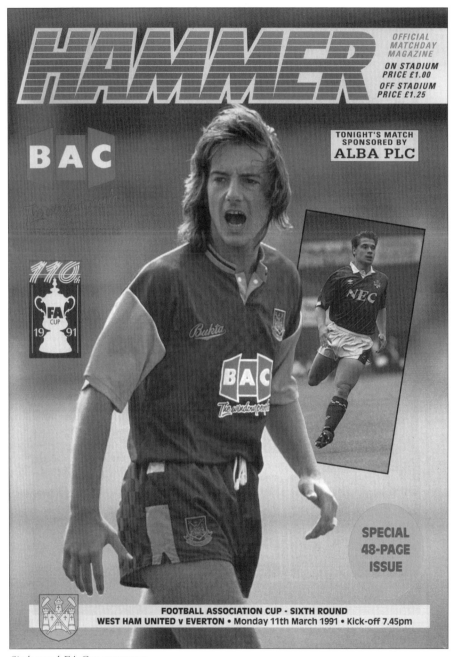

*Sixth round FA Cup programme.*

*Tickets for the Sixth round FA Cup game.*

manager himself. Miklosko was reliable in goal and Tony Gale was an effective stopper. In midfield Steve Potts was inexhaustible, and Ian Bishop, a Macari signing, was a good passer of the ball and the main playmaker. Up front Quinn and McAvennie provided a modest goal threat.

There was one player in the side who definitely had the potential to become a West Ham legend. Stuart Slater was a product of West Ham's famed Academy, and as a youngster he was regarded as a star in the making. He signed as a professional at 17, and generated real excitement, in the way Joe Cole did when he appeared for the first team. That night against Everton at Upton Park the young winger showed just how good a player he was. He simply tore the Toffees' defence to shreds.

The Hammers went at their opponents straight from the kick-off, and it was no surprise when Bonds' side went ahead. In the 35th minute, after long periods when they totally dominated, Colin Foster fired a volley past Neville Southall to put his side into a well-deserved lead. A bedraggled Everton side could not cope with the Hammers' sustained attacking play and were relieved to go in at half-time only one goal down. At the interval the home crowd stood to applaud their team's superb performance, with young Slater singled out for special praise.

With the home crowd in full voice and Slater continuing to run rampant down the right side, the Hammers started the second period like an express train. The winger began to instill panic in the Everton defence every time he touched the ball. Then, in the 60th minute, he announced his arrival in the top flight with the most sublime piece of skill. With the Everton defence helpless to intervene, the sensational Slater raced down the wing, skipped past two feeble challenges, turned inside and hit a crisp, low shot into the corner of the net past the helpless Southall.

Two goals up and in sizzling form, the Hammers ran the remainder of the game, with Bishop and Potts pulling the strings in midfield. But the real star of the night was the goalscoring Academy boy, who received a tremendous ovation as he left the field at the final whistle. He had put West Ham into the semi-final of the FA Cup, and the fans loved him for it.

Howard Kendall brought on ex-Hammer Tony Cottee, and Everton scored a late goal from Dave Watson, but it was too little, too late for the Merseysiders. The Hammers were safely through to the semi-final and 90 minutes from Wembley. After the game Kendall spoke glowingly of the Hammers' young man of the match: 'Stuart Slater was the difference between the sides.'

Suffolk-born Stuart Slater made his debut in 1986 and played 141 games for the Hammers before he was sold to Celtic in 1992 for £1.5 million. He represented England at Under-21 level and for the B side, but this was a miserable haul for a player of Slater's huge potential. By his own omission, the FA Cup victory over Everton in 1991 was the high point in his career. Slater also later admitted that his move to Celtic was ill-advised. He revealed on his website that 'the saddest moment of my football career was leaving West Ham to join Celtic in 1992.'

The dazzling winger was honest to admit that he listened too much to his agent, when all he really wanted was to stay at Upton Park. He admitted, 'I had a huge price tag pinned on my head...West Ham made their best-ever offer, yet my agent just looked back across the desk and said no. I was not strong enough to say I wanted to sign. I probably would've stayed and been a one-team man.'

Never one of Alan Curbishley's overpaid and underachieving 'Bentley Boys', the popular Slater is now back at West Ham working hard behind the scenes.

Buoyed by Slater's match-winning performance against Everton, the Hammers headed for Villa Park for the semi-final against Nottingham Forest in rare high spirits. But 1991 was not to be their year as Forest ran out easy winners by the emphatic score-line of 4–0. It didn't help the Hammers' cause that centre-half Tony Gale was controversially sent-off, but in truth, they were outclassed by a superbly organised Forest side.

Billy Bonds would not have been happy with the Forest semi-final result, but his team had reached the last four of the FA Cup and were still in the running for an automatic promotion spot. They eventually achieved promotion but lasted just one season in Division One. The Hammers bounced back into the Premier League, the new promised land of English football, in 1992. That was when the trouble started.

As the Hammers returned to the radically revamped top flight, Bonds was confronted with the most tumultuous off-field drama the club had faced in years. West Ham United was in chaos and the furious fans in an angry mood. To meet the recommendations of the Taylor Report, the board introduced a Bond Scheme, which came to be as loathed as much as Thatcher's despised Poll Tax. The scheme was introduced as a way of funding the ground development made compulsory by Lord Justice Taylor's report into the Hillsborough tragedy and ground safety in general. All League clubs were required to tear down their outdated concrete structures and replace them with all-seater stadia, complete with luxury boxes and facilities for corporate entertainment. Redeveloping football stadia in inner-city areas like Upton Park was beyond the modest means of clubs like West Ham. The Bonds Scheme was the board's preferred way to raise the funds required for modernisation, but it was an ill-conceived venture from the start. The scheme involved fans securing their seats at discount prices on a long-term basis in return for a down payment of a non-returnable £500. The fans saw through the scheme, with its minimal guarantee for future season tickets. Managing director Peter Storrie was given the job of selling the scheme to the fans by chairman Terry Brown. The fans reviled Brown for his part in the affair and his callous treatment of some of the most loyal followers in the English game. Both Brown and Storrie left the club a few years later, and West Ham was well rid of the pair of them.

Season-ticket holders turned their backs on the scheme, which was drastically under-subscribed. They staged a series of protests, pitch invasions and other demonstrations of their anger. One result of their insurrection was an alarming fall in attendances at the Boleyn, further contributing to the club's financial problems. This was the backdrop to West Ham in the early 1990s and the appalling context for Billy Bonds' side's return to the top flight. What should have been one of the most important periods in the history of the club had been reduced to chaos by an impatient and money-grabbing board of directors.

The incident destroyed the players' morale, and the ultimate effect was that the Hammers were relegated again. The immensely popular Bonds was visibly shaken by the self-inflicted problems at the club and brought in his old teammate, Harry Redknapp, to share the load. The duo developed a strong partnership and quickly achieved promotion and their place in the Premier League. The fans must have been giddy with all this coming and going, and they were desperate for some stability.

Amid the political and financial mayhem at the club and its effect on the performance of the players, the news broke in February 1993 of the death of Bobby Moore. The shock was felt throughout the nation, but around Upton Park there was an atmosphere of extreme desolation and disbelief.

The public response to Moore's death was frankly unexpected. Nobody could remember such an emotional outburst of public affection for a sporting figure. At West Ham the response was immediate, as thousands of fans and well-wishers made the pilgrimage to the Boleyn Ground to pay their respects and say goodbye. Shirts, scarves, messages, wreaths and flowers adorned the gates to the ground, which became a shrine to his memory. Visitors to Upton Park stood in stunned silence at the sight of the gates, which by this time were a sea of claret and blue. Complete strangers wept in each other's arms, overcome with emotion and a profound sense of loss. As one fan said at the time, 'Bobby's death rocked the country…you just don't see scenes of public unity like this today.'

To achieve this kind of emotional outpouring there had to be something about Bobby Moore that transcended football. Certainly, he was hugely popular during his life, but the level of grief even surprised his wife, Stephanie, who said, 'What was very supportive was that the entire nation mourned, and it was only then that I realised what a legend he was.'

Moore's death put everything into perspective at West Ham. With old Hammers like Bonds and Redknapp in charge, the club enjoyed a settled spell in the Premier League in the 1990s. This rare period of calm in the club's recent history saw a return to some of the old values. It was as though the loss of their greatest player inspired the club to respect its past.

Despite all the problems, the sixth-round FA Cup victory against Everton in 1991, the performance of Stuart Slater and the promotion to the Premier League were signs that the Hammers remained capable of competing with the best teams in England.

**Final score: West Ham United 2 Everton 1**
West Ham United:

# 24.

# WEST HAM UNITED

# V TOTTENHAM HOTSPUR

## FA CARLING PREMIERSHIP    11 MARCH 1997

The relationship between West Ham and Millwall resembles two pitbull terriers in mortal combat. The intense hatred between the two sets of supporters is rooted in local history. The clubs have their origins in the local iron industry, and the rivalry is said to have started in the 1920s when the workers from Millwall Ironworks on the Isle of Dogs refused to support their striking colleagues in Canning Town. Down the years West Ham's promotion to the First Division has often been at the expense of their local rivals, adding to the strength of the enmity.

The West Ham/Millwall rivalry is one of the most notorious within the whole world of football hooliganism. When the teams were drawn again each other in the second round of League Cup on 25 August 2009, violent clashes between hundreds of fans were seen in the streets around Upton Park for the first time in many years. Fighting erupted in the ground during the match, and there were several unwelcome pitch invasions. The clubs had not played each other for four years, and it was a warning to the smug football authorities that serious trouble is never far away in matches between intense rivals. Fortunately, there were no fatalities.

The games against Tottenham are tame affairs in comparison, although rivalry between the two clubs has been fuelled by the transfers of Paul Allen, Jermaine Defoe and repeated rumours of Tottenham courting the Hammers' best player of 2010, Scott Parker. West Ham fans will always believe that the Spurs manager, Harry Redknapp, born a stone's throw from Upton Park, is claret and blue at heart. The two clubs certainly have history.

The Premiership derby against Tottenham at Upton Park on February 1997 was a crucial one for the Hammers, and it is memorable for all the right reasons. The club had enjoyed a decent run in the new Premier League under Redknapp, regularly finishing in mid-table, but their fortunes began to take a dive when they lost at home

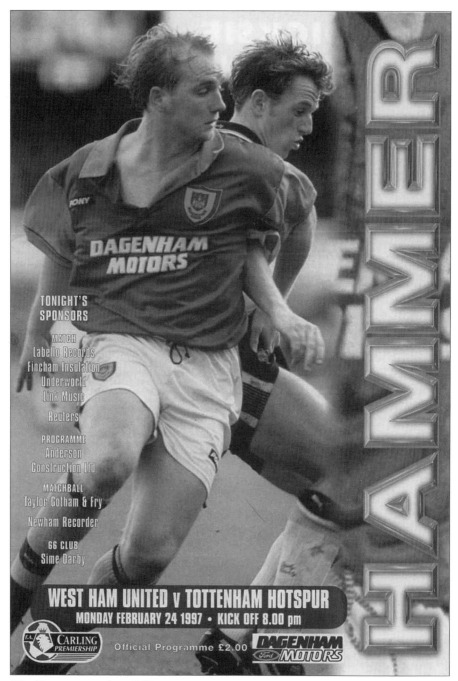

*West Ham programme from 1997.*

**WEST HAM UNITED PLC**

F.A. CARLING PREMIERSHIP
WEST HAM UNITED -V- TOTTENHAM
SAT 22 FEB 1997  KICK OFF 15:00P.M.

**NL2**

# CENTENARY STAND LOWER

ROW   SEAT   PRICE
C     87     £22.00

ENTER VIA STILES 1-7 IN GREEN ST (AWAY FANS)
130197 TOTTENHAM HOTSPUR F.C.
TO BE RETAINED UNTIL END OF MATCH

*Home ticket for the match against Tottenham Hotspur.*

to Wrexham in the third round of the FA Cup. The humiliating defeat exposed serious weaknesses of both ability and attitude, and not for the first time the Hammers were the subject of an embarrassing act of giant-killing.

Spurs came to the match at Upton Park with players of the quality of Campbell, Sheringham, Anderton and Gerry Francis in their side, but they had managerial problems of their own. Despite this they would have gained confidence in knowing the Hammers were involved in a white knuckle relegation ride. They had not won in 10 games and were a worrying 17th in the League.

In a last-ditch, desperate bid to avoid the drop, Redknapp made two major signings that year, which transformed their season. John Hartson was a burly, aggressive centre-forward who must have been a nightmare to defend against. His wholehearted approach to the game endeared him to the North Bank. His fellow new boy, Paul Kitson, was an unlikely hero. A stylish player with a deceptively casual look about him, the cultured striker struck up a devastating partnership with Hartson that turned the team's fortunes.

Hartson and Kitson proved to be Redknapp's get-out-of-jail card – if we can use that phrase about the wheeler-dealer former West Ham boss. The pair's 13 goals that season kept the Hammers up, and the pair they scored against Tottenham were the start of the spree.

The atmosphere at the Boleyn was edgy as the two teams emerged from the tunnel in the pouring rain. With their confidence low after a poor run, the team needed the fans to be at their magnificent best. The side for this match had the experience of Julian Dicks, Steve Moncur and Steve Potts, the raw promise of Rio Ferdinand and the superb goalkeeping of Ludo Miklosko. Ian Bishop was a creative and classy midfield player in the true traditions of the club, and the young, if still podgy, Frank Lampard Jnr was on the bench if required. But the £7 million striking duo were the heroes that Monday night as the Hammers tore into their North London rivals.

The match got off to the worst possible start for the home side. After just eight minutes the Hammers' hopes were dashed as Sheringham's freakish long-range header from Carr's cross was picked up by the strong wind and looped over Miklosko into the net. Fortunately for the home-side, skipper Julian Dicks was in no mood for yet another miserable evening. His muscular long throw defied the wind, but Campbell was on hand to head the ball out for a corner. Michael Hughes took the kick and Dicks was the first to react, directing his header firmly into the net to level the score.

Urged on by their fans, the Hammers surged forward, and Kitson, with a diving header, gave his team the lead with their second goal inside two minutes. The home side were coping better with the strong wind, playing in neat triangles and jealously guarding possession.

The wind seemed to gain in strength and heavily influenced the next goal. Darren Anderton hardly had a touch in the first 45 minutes, but in a rare Spurs attack, the winger strode forward, and his intended chip over Miklosko was going well wide until the wind picked up the ball and directed it straight into the net. Spurs were encouraged by the goal and slowly fought their way back into what was becoming a very scrappy affair.

The Hammers refused to allow Spurs to gain the upper hand, with Potts and Bishop working hard to control midfield. Julian Dicks seemed to be everywhere – quite an achievement for a left-back. Late in the half, with the scores level, Dicks drove a free-kick into the Spurs penalty area, where Hartson out-jumped Campbell and headed in at the far post. The noise from the North Bank was deafening as the home side ended the first half well on top and with the cushion of a one-goal lead.

Upton Park fell silent in the 53rd minute, however, when a clever Sheringham lay-off released Howells, who, under intense pressure from Ferdinand, somehow slid the ball into the net to level the scores. As Potts and Bishop began to tire in the conditions, Spurs started to dominate possession with their intricate passing and movement off the ball, but the Hammers' defence remained solid with Dicks, roared on by the North Bank, performing outstandingly.

The decisive moment of the match occurred in the 72nd minute when Kitson flicked on Breaker's free-kick. Hartson was first to the knock-down and looked certain to score when he was dragged down by Howells. Man of the match Dicks stepped up and rifled a ferocious penalty past Walker. Surely this time the Irons would hold on to their 4–3 lead?

The Spurs players looked deflated and appeared to run out of steam and ideas in the last 15 minutes. The Hammers held on to record their second Premiership win in five months. Goals from Hartson and Kitson, and the heroics of Julian Dicks, allowed West Ham to escape relegation by a mere two points, although their tally of 42 would have brought them safety in any other season.

Today, nobody remembers Harry Redknapp as the dashing young winger at Upton Park in the 1960s. Redknapp is now famous as a successful, if controversial, manager of a succession of clubs, including his treasured West Ham United. Redknapp was the club's manager from 1994 to 2001, winning the Intertoto Cup and achieving a highly creditable fifth place in the League.

Redknapp joined the club as assistant manager to Billy Bonds, but he emerged as the stronger character and, under highly contentious circumstances, was appointed manager at the beginning of the 1994–95 season. Bonds was kicked upstairs, as the saying goes, and offered a job as director of football. Understandably, the West Ham legend took offence and resigned immediately.

The fans, who never really took to Redknapp, despite his Hammers pedigree, organised a mass protest to express their disgust at yet another callous decision by the board of directors. Bonds was revered at Upton Park – only Bobby Moore was held in greater esteem. Most fans wanted Bonds to remain as manager and believed that Redknapp had betrayed his close friend. The two mates, West Ham through and through, fell out over the incident and did not speak again for years.

In time, Redknapp gained the respect of the fans as he turned the team from a relegation nightmare to mid-table respectability. However, controversy is rarely far away with Redknapp, and a few unguarded remarks to a fanzine editor enraged his chairman, who demanded an immediate explanation. Unconvinced by his manager's story, Brown sacked Redknapp on the spot. That was the end of his long and thorny relationship with West Ham as player, coach and manager.

The row with Brown was essentially about the sale of Frank Lampard to Chelsea. Redknapp had worked hard to rebuild the Academy tradition with stunning results. Rio Ferdinand, Michael Carrick, Joe Cole, Glen Johnson, and Frank Lampard all came through the ranks during Redknapp's reign at West Ham. He was right to be furious as he saw the greatest array of young talent for two generations about to be sold to the highest bidder.

In 1997, with the team in trouble, Redknapp and the fans knew the importance of staying in the Premier League. It meant the Sky TV jackpot could be used to acquire experienced players to support the youngsters. As a direct result of the Sky largesse, the club had a few good years, ultimately leading to a return to European football. These were happy days at Upton Park, and they began with Hartson and Kitson and the crucial win over Tottenham on that wet and windy Monday night in February. The Hammers finished the season in 14th place, and they used their survival to good effect, achieving top-10 finishes in the next few seasons.

**Final score: West Ham United 4 Tottenham Hotspur 3**
West Ham United: Miklosko, Breacker, Dicks, Potts, Ferdinand, Bowen, Moncur, Hughes, Bishop, Hartson, Kitson.
Substitutes: Dowie (78).

# 25.

# WEST HAM UNITED
# V MIDDLESBOROUGH

## FA CARLING PREMIERSHIP          16 MAY 1999

$A$ West Ham Premier League fixture against the Middlesborough team of the 1990s is a surprise candidate for a memorable match, but this one was different. The match turned out to be one of the most important of the Redknapp era. The Hammers had ended the 1997–98 campaign in eighth place, and hopes were high for a title challenge the following season, or at least a top-five finish.

After a few years of mid-table mediocrity, Redknapp and his assistant, Frank Lampard Snr, improved the side to such an extent that they began to compete on equal terms with the likes of Manchester United, Liverpool and Arsenal. Competing with the rich clubs at the top of the table is always going to be tough for clubs like West Ham, but Redknapp showed that, with some shrewd signings, a good youth policy and commitment from the players, it could be done.

The team for the Boro match had one familiar name in Steve Potts, and Rio Ferdinand and Frank Lampard Jnr had established themselves in the side, but Redknapp realised he had to strengthen the team if they were to be serious contenders for major honours. He brought in the former Liverpool and Tottenham defender 'Razor' Ruddock to provide some muscle to a lightweight defence, and the Israeli international Eyal Berkovic restored real quality to the Hammers' midfield, absent since the Brooking/Devonshire partnership.

With Ferdinand's pace and Ruddock's experience, the defence looked solid. The Lampard/Berkovic

*Home ticket for the Bobby Moore Stand.*

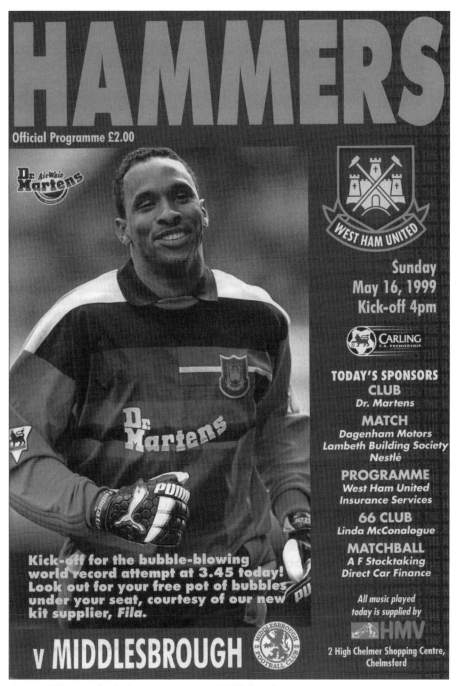

*A copy of Hammers for the League game against Middlesbrough,*

midfield combination was as good as any in the Premier League. Both were attacking players who could score goals from midfield, and both knew how to keep the ball. With Trevor Sinclair, a £1.6 million signing from Queen's Park Rangers, adding pace and skill down the right, the midfield was the best seen at the Boleyn for years. Redknapp had assembled a good blend of youth and experience, and more importantly they could all play, with the possible exception of Ruddock, whose best days were clearly behind him. In fairness to the centre-half, Redknapp praised Ruddock for his positive influence in training and on the pitch. Razor's insistence on playing Elvis Presley records before matches may not have impressed the youngsters in the side, but it injected some much needed life into the Hammers' dressing room.

South-London born Ruddock was a complex character. He had famously wound up Patrick Viera in a match against Arsenal, with Viera retaliating by spitting in Ruddock's face, which resulted in a nine-day ban for the Frenchman. The aggressive 6ft 2in centre-half had weight problems through his career, perhaps the reason why he only made one appearance for England, when Terry Venables selected him for a match against Nigeria. But Ruddock did a good job for Redknapp, as the manager knew he would.

Up front the Hammers had Marc Keller alongside Ian Wright, signed from Arsenal in the summer of 1998. Wright, who was not in the side for the Middlesborough game, had a difficult time at Upton Park, which included a suspension for trashing the referee's dressing room after being sent off in a home game against Leeds United. He was later awarded an MBE for services to football.

Redknapp and Lampard Snr's man-management skills were tested to the full as they set out to build this bunch of strong and difficult players into a cohesive unit. It is to their credit that they succeeded, more or less. This was a very good West Ham side, and one that excited the often hard-to-please Upton Park crowd. Redknapp knew he had something with this team and that the fans could relax with little fear of relegation. Joe Cole was breaking through, but he was still very young. The manager knew his team needed something a bit special, and he found it in Paolo Di Canio.

The controversial Italian was an inspired signing, and he won over the Hammers supporters from the moment he arrived at the Boleyn. They worshipped him for his magical skill and passionate commitment to the team, and he proved to be Redknapp's missing ingredient.

There have been few more controversial figures in football than Paolo Di Canio. After a career that saw him move between clubs in Serie A, the difficult-to-handle Di Canio was sold by AC Milan to Celtic by Fabio Capello. He scored 15 goals in 36 games for Celtic but was sold to Sheffield Wednesday the following season. The wandering star left Wednesday for West Ham in January 1999, helping the club to qualify for the UEFA Cup. He scored 48 goals in 118 matches for the Hammers, some of which were the most spectacular in the Premier League. However, following a spat with Glenn Roeder, Redknapp's successor, the hot-headed Italian was eventually sold to Charlton before he returned to his beloved Lazio. Di Canio never played for Italy, unbelievable for such a great player. He fell out with most of his managers, including Capello, Ron Atkinson and Marcello Lippi – perhaps he was just too hot to handle.

Always close to the extreme right-wing Lazio supporters, the notorious Irriducibili, Di Canio raised his arm in a Nazi salute after he scored a wonder goal for Lazio against Roma in 2005. He also had 'DVX' tattooed on his arm, a Latin expression used by the Italian dictator Mussolini. None of this endeared him to his managers. But there were at least two sides to the mercurial forward. Di Canio was awarded the FIFA Fair Play Award in 2001 following an incident at Goodison Park. In a match against Everton the Italian stunned the West Ham fans when, instead of rolling the ball into an empty net, Di Canio stopped play by catching the ball when he spotted the Everton goalkeeper lying badly injured. Di Canio could have simply walked the ball into the net. Harry Redknapp said Di Canio 'does things with the ball that make you gasp. Other footballers would pay to watch him train.'

In 1999 the consummate football entertainer scored what most commentators consider to be the greatest goal ever scored in the Premier League. His strike, a sublime volley against Wimbledon, was voted BBC Goal of the Season and is immortalised forever on YouTube.

Di Canio was in the side to play Middlesborough that May, and he was at his inspirational best. Having spent most of the season in the dizzy heights of the top end of the table, the Hammers hadn't lost their inbred ability to self-destruct. They had been soundly beaten in their previous two games, having suffered a 6–0 defeat at the hands of Everton at Goodison Park before being annihilated 5–1 by Leeds United at Upton Park. Clearly Redknapp and Lampard still had work to do.

The atmosphere at the Boleyn was tense when Boro arrived for the final game of the season. West Ham needed victory to qualify for a place in the UEFA Cup. However, this depended on Arsenal beating Aston Villa across London at Highbury. In the corresponding fixture the previous season, the Midlanders had beaten Arsenal to deny the Hammers a place in Europe, so the crowd knew what was at stake. They were nervous and edgy, but, led by the North Bank, they quickly got behind their team.

The crowd begun to relax and enjoy themselves after Frank Lampard Jnr crashed in a shot in the fourth minute. The young midfielder was to repeat his goal many times in his career, but this was a crucial one for his team. Local lad Lampard played well that day, but he was never popular with the Upton Park crowd. Many thought he was overweight and only in the team because his dad was assistant manager. The truth is that he was a huge talent who was never at his best in a claret-and-blue shirt, which he was soon to discard in favour of Chelsea blue.

Marc Keller added a second just before the break, tapping in from close range. Redknapp's team-talk couldn't have been easier – more of the same please lads! The home side comfortably saw out the remainder of the half and were applauded loudly from the pitch by their faithful fans.

The Hammers came out for the second half in a determined mood, playing some delightful football and continuing to threaten the Boro goal. The home crowd relaxed a little when news came through from Highbury that Kanu had put the Gunners ahead. Spurred on by the news, Trevor Sinclair quickly made it three. The winger was a real hit at Upton Park, and his good form was rewarded with an England cap. Sadly, he was later sold to Manchester City in the fire sale of the club's greatest talent, along with Lampard, Carrick, Ferdinand, Cole, James and Defoe.

The Sinclair goal put the crowd in celebratory mood, and the party really got going when Di Canio joined in the fun, finishing from close range to make it four. The news from Highbury lifted the mood even higher – Villa had lost and the Hammers achieved their highest League position since 1986, finishing in a giddy fifth place.

The Middlesborough match was crucial for the Hammers because, for the first time in their history, the club had qualified for Europe through a League position. There was a small downside in that they were not eligible for an automatic UEFA Cup place but needed to qualify through the Intertoto Cup. The competition was played in the middle of summer, when most Premier League players were sunning themselves on the beaches of the Caribbean. But West Ham were back in Europe, and their fans could begin to dream.

**Final score: West Ham United 4 Middlesborough 0**

West Ham United: Forrest, Potts, Ruddock, Ferdinand, Minto, Berkovic, Lampard, Foe, Keller, Di Canio, Sinclair.

Substitutes: Cole (83).

# 26.

# WEST HAM UNITED

# V FC METZ

## UEFA INTERTOTO CUP FINAL,

## SECOND LEG                    24 AUGUST 1999

Having finished the League in fifth place, Harry Redknapp was unhappy that his team had not qualified automatically for the UEFA Cup. The Intertoto Cup was regarded as a bit of a joke, played by teams from Latvia, Lithuania, Luxembourg and sometimes Fulham. But Redknapp was a realist and understood that the Intertoto provided a back door into the UEFA Cup. He also knew it would take six games to make this a reality.

These were happy days for Hammers supporters, back in Europe for the first time in a generation and riding high in the League. Holiday plans were swiftly rearranged when the fixtures for the Intertoto Cup were announced.

The Hammers' first competitive fixture in 1999–2000 was the first-round match on the 7 July against the unlikely named Finish side FC Jokerit. Despite the midsummer start to the season, Redknapp's team progressed smoothly to the Final, easily overcoming Jokerit and Holland's Heerenveen. The final against FC Metz was a much tougher task. The match was memorable because it put West Ham back in the big time of European football for the first time in over 30 years.

The French side arrived at Upton Park for the first leg hoping for a

*Ticket for the first leg of the 1999 Intertoto Cup.*

165

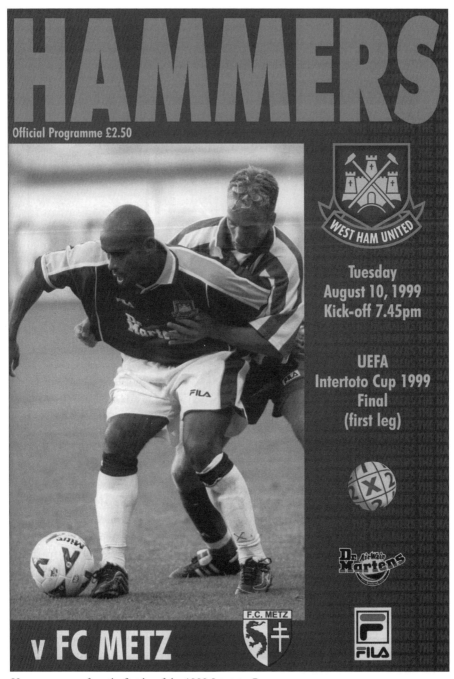

*Home programme from the first leg of the 1999 Intertoto Cup.*

*Ticket from the Second leg which West Ham needed to score with two away goals to avoid penalties.*

draw, but against the odds they won 1–0, with Frank Lampard Jnr missing a penalty to level the scores. Some things never change! Despite the reverse, thousands of Irons supporters made their way across the channel for the second leg to cheer their team to a place in the UEFA Cup.

The Hammers needed at least two away goals to avoid the nail-biting situation of a penalty shoot-out. Their travelling fans were rewarded when their team wiped out the deficit before half-time. In the 23rd minute Trevor Sinclair turned onto a dream of a pass from Di Canio and buried his shot into the corner of the net. The French crowd were forced to listen to a raucous rendition of Bubbles as the away supporters demanded a second goal. They did not have to wait long. With Redknapp preparing his team-talk on the Hammers' bench, his team scored again. Young Lampard made amends for his first-leg penalty miss with a well-taken goal just two minutes before the break.

The Hammers supporters sang their hearts out during the interval, confident they had a full European season to look forward to. But the French side came out for the second half all-guns blazing and in no mood to surrender. They silenced the noisy Hammers fans when Jestrovic scored

*Teamsheets from the second leg.*

*Samassi Abou and Trevor Sinclair celebrate after the Hammers beat Metz in August 1999.*

with 20 minutes to go, putting the result back in the balance and setting up a tense finish. There was nothing to choose between the teams at this stage, and extra-time looked the most likely outcome until the Hammers scored a goal that deserved to take them into the UEFA Cup.

With Lampard, Lomas and Moncur beginning to get the edge in midfield, Paulo Wanchope broke away, rounded the French 'keeper and calmly slid the ball into the net. Metz were beaten and Lampard was spared the embarrassment of the penalty shoot-out.

Wanchope was an interesting player. Redknapp acquired the Costa Rican from Derby County largely on the basis of his wonder goal against Manchester United when he beat four defenders before squeezing the ball past the United 'keeper. Wanchope scored 28 goals in 79 games for Derby but never really settled at Upton Park, where he managed just 15 goals in 46 games. He was later sold to Manchester City. Despite his modest show in English football, the centre-forward became a cult figure in his native Costa Rica, and he is their greatest-ever goalscorer.

Wanchope's goal against Metz was his most important for the Hammers. It not only won a Cup Final but put his club into the draw for the UEFA Cup first round. Redknapp's decision to enter the competition was thoroughly justified.

West Ham had won the Intertoto Cup, and their fans celebrated on their way back across the channel, but the match had never felt like a European Final, with its two-leg format and tiny grounds. The presentation was a farce, and the players and fans knew that they hadn't really won a Cup but simply qualified for the real thing.

Now they could look forward to the new season with a real sense of excitement and join Juventus, Tottenham, Arsenal and old friends Anderlecht in the UEFA Cup.

The Hammers finished ninth in the Premier League in the 1999–2000 season but were disappointing in the Cup competitions. In time-honoured tradition, they lost 1–0 away to Tranmere Rovers in the third round of the FA Cup and their UEFA Cup journey ended in second-round defeat at the hands of Steaua Bucharest. The hope and anticipation the fans felt in August ended in frustration and anger.

Redknapp moved on in 2001, his place taken by Glenn Roeder, who stepped up from his position as youth-team manager at Upton Park. Roeder was an honest, hard-working young manager, and his team achieved a highly creditable seventh-place finish in his first season in charge. Unfortunately for Roeder, the Hammers were relegated to the Championship at the end of the following season.

Roeder's team were relegated with 42 points, the highest gained by a relegated team. Trevor Brooking stepped in for the final few games in place of Roeder, who was struggling with serious health problems. Even the legendary Brooking couldn't inspire the side, and they went down following a disappointing 2–2 draw with Birmingham City.

West Ham were relegated just a few seasons after qualifying for Europe and years of top-10 finishes in the Premier League. The club had a sparkling, revamped ground and squad of players that should have been challenging for the Premiership title. Cole, Carrick, Defoe, Johnson, Sinclair, James, Kanouté and Di Canio are the guilty names and were all regular members of the side of 2002–03. Lampard, Dicks and Ferdinand had already left, and the others were soon to follow – all gone within a year in a fire sale, held to pay off some of the club's mounting pile of debt.

The promising young Reading manager Alan Pardew arrived in October 2003 as Roeder's replacement, and it took the unassuming Pardew two seasons to get the club back to the Premiership. At the end of the new manager's first season the Hammers made the Play-off Final, only to lose 1–0 to Crystal Palace. A year later they were back at the Millennium Stadium, this time with Preston North End as their Play-off Final opponents.

**Final score: FC Metz 1 West Ham United 3**
West Ham United: Hislop, Ferdinand, Lomas, Potts, Sinclair, Lampard, Foe, Keller, Moncur, Di Canio, Wanchope.
Substitutes: Cole (for Di Canio, 78).

# 27.

# WEST HAM UNITED

# V PRESTON NORTH END

## CHAMPIONSHIP PLAY-OFF FINAL    30 MAY 2005

One of the Hammers' most endearing qualities is the ability to bounce back to the top flight after just a season or two in the Championship. A year or two out of the Premier League should have given the club and fans an opportunity to regroup and reassess their priorities, but that was not the case here. The West Ham fans are notoriously impatient and demanding, as new manager Alan Pardew was to learn. Pardew's first task could not have been more challenging – to win over the fans by getting the team back up at the first attempt. He achieved the first step in making the Play-offs in 2003–04.

In May 2004 the Hammers faced Ipswich in the semi-finals with the first leg at Portman Road, never an easy place to visit. Joe Royle's side were a solid outfit with a dangerous centre-forward in Darren Bent. Pardew knew his players had to be disciplined and well-organised if they had any chance of making the Final. The manager would have been delighted with his team's performance on the immaculate pitch until Bent headed Ipswich into the lead in the second half. Roared on by the home crowd, Ipswich went looking for the crucial second goal, but the Hammers defended well for the rest of the game, keeping the score down to a single goal at the end of the first leg.

The second leg at Upton Park was memorable both for the match and the atmosphere that night under the Boleyn floodlights. It was one of the most electrifying nights ever experienced at the ground. Many of us could not remember a night like it since the glory days of the 1960s. Ipswich must have wondered what had hit them when they strolled out onto the Upton Park cauldron.

The sides were evenly matched and something special would be required from the Hammers if they were to penetrate the strong Ipswich defence and level the score. Sure enough, it came in the second half when winger Matty Etherington accepted a short corner from Carrick, moved a couple of paces forward and smacked the ball into the top corner of the net. What a goal!

With the Hammers fan hollering Bubbles at the top of their voices, Christian Dailly, up in the penalty area in a desperate attempt to force the second goal, stabbed the ball in from close range. The Scot then collapsed in pain from a knock in the most sensitive region of his anatomy. But the injury didn't stop him from celebrating his goal when he realised what he had done for his team. The ground went crazy at the final whistle. The Hammers were on their way to the Millennium Stadium and, fingers crossed, back to where they belonged – the Premier League.

The Millennium Stadium brought heartbreak for the Hammers fans. They had watched their side give everything against Ipswich in the semi-final, only to see them fall at the last hurdle. The Premier League was snatched away from them on the last day of the season.

The Hammers travelled to Cardiff confident in the belief that they were a better side than their opponents, Crystal Palace. In truth they were a better side than Palace but not that day. The South Londoners won thanks to a second-half Neil Shipperley goal. On the day of the Final, when it really mattered, the Hammers were a pale shadow of the side that had defeated Ipswich in the semi-final. Cardiff was the site of mixed fortunes for the Hammers over the next few years – but in the 2004 Play-off Final the dream died for another year.

The next season there was no alternative than try to do it all again. After a difficult 2004–05, United made it to the Play-offs for the second year running. A terrific away win at Watford on the final day of the season secured their place in the semi-final, where their opponents were again Ipswich Town.

Ipswich, denied the previous year, had led the table for most of the season. The Hammers, who had only finished in sixth place, welcomed the Tractor Boys to Upton Park for the first leg and got off to the perfect start. Marlon Harewood gave the home side a seventh-minute lead, and Bobby Zamora made it two only six minutes later. Spurred on by a ferocious home crowd, the Hammers were in sensational form. Michael Carrick was at his best and controlled the midfield with a calm authority, unusual in one so young. He was definitely beginning to look the finished article.

Unfortunately, Ipswich pulled one back before the break, just as the crowd were beginning to relax. Gaining in confidence, the Tractor Boys stunned the home supporters by grabbing an equaliser. Nothing is ever simple with the Hammers, and they still had everything to do at this stage of the tie.

The atmosphere at the start of the second game at Portman Road was excruciatingly tense, but Bobby Zamora stepped up to earn his place in the Hammers' history books. The centre-forward, who had been disappointing since his move to Upton Park, scored twice. The second goal was an absolute stunner, and it secured his side a place in the Championship Play-off Final. The fans returned to Cardiff for the second time in two years.

They say there is no greater prize in football than winning the Championship Play-off Final and a place in the Premier League. West Ham simply could not afford to lose for a second time. Their opponents at Cardiff were Preston, the club's opponents back in 1964, when Bobby Moore lifted the FA Cup for the first time in the club's history. Preston would have revelled in being the underdogs to the East Londoners, who would have felt the pressure of being favourites. In addition, the Hammers must have felt some anxiety about returning to the ground where they were beaten the previous season.

Pardew was able to field the same team that beat Ipswich in the semi-final, and most of the Hammers' hopes were centred on the striking partnership of Zamora and Harewood and the threat from the left wing of the excellent Matthew Etherington. With Reo-Coker and Mullins in midfield, the team had a solid look, while the defensive partnership of the tough Tomas Repka and the classy Anton Ferdinand was growing in authority.

Aware of the magnitude of the occasion, the Hammers started strongly, with Etherington going close and Repka hitting a post with a speculative effort. But as both teams settled, the game became a tactical battle with neither team prepared to commit too many players forward. The Hammers enjoyed most of the possession in the first half but failed to penetrate the superbly organised Preston defence. At this stage the feeling in the stadium was that whoever scored first would win the game.

The Irons had the better of the first half but failed to score, and at half-time the teams remained level. At the interval it was the claret-and-blue section of the ground that was feeling nervous.

Pardew's half-time talk must have calmed his players. They started the second period in fine style, with Harewood and Zamora both wasting glorious chances to put their team ahead. The two Hammers' forwards had a habit of blowing good opportunities, and the fans must have wondered if this really was going to be their day. Preston had less of the ball but still managed to put pressure on Walker in the United goal.

Suddenly the game changed. Matty Etherington, as he had done all afternoon, raced down the left-wing and delivered the perfect cross to Zamora. The previously wasteful centre-forward was first to the ball and crashed a shot over the Preston 'keeper and into the net, sending the Hammers supporters into seventh heaven.

It was due reward for the Irons, who had provided the best attacking moments of the match. At the heart of their offensive play was the irrepressible Etherington. He was a good buy for West Ham, and why he was later sold to Stoke City we will never know. He went on to be the Potteries' Player of the Year in 2009, and the Hammers had lost yet another outstanding talent.

Bobby Zamora was to be the hero of the hour. Goalkeeper Walker had to be replaced by Stephen Bywater when, late in the game, he twisted an ankle going for a Stoke cross. Pardew brought on Christian Dailly and the youngster Mark Noble for the last 15 minutes in a bid to preserve his side's narrow lead. But, as hard as Preston fought, they could not find a way through the Hammers' defence. The final whistle sounded, sending the claret-and-blue players and fans into raptures of delight. You could feel the relief on the pitch and all the way round the West Ham end of the stadium.

Alan Pardew and his players had won the Championship Play-off Final and were back in the Premier League. With claret-and-blue scarves flying from car windows, the West Ham contingent made their way back along the M4 in high spirits as they contemplated life back in the big time. They would be satisfied with an eighth-place finish in the Premier League the following season, but would have hardly dreamed they would be back in the Welsh capital 12 months later, this time in the Final of the FA Cup.

**Final score: West Ham United 1 Preston North End 0**

West Ham United: Walker, Repka, Ferdinand, Ward, Powell, Newton, Mullins, Reo-Coker, Etherington, Harewood, Zamora.

Substitutes: Bywater (for Walker, 87), Noble (for Newton, 82), Dailly (for Zamora 74).

# 28.

# WEST HAM UNITED

# V LIVERPOOL

## FA CUP FINAL                    13 MAY 2006

Ian Drury wrote a song called Madly in Love with Pandora, in which the Essex man sings about the ups and downs of family life in his Essex home. West Ham fans would sympathise with Drury's sentiments as they watched their beloved club suffer the ups and downs of relegation and promotion, with the odd Cup run thrown in for light relief.

Following John Lyall's brutal sacking in 1989, the club had six months with someone called Lou Macari before Billy Bonds and Harry Redknapp brought some sort of order and tradition back to the club. Glenn Roeder was an honest man but over-promoted, and in any case he had serious health problems. Most fans wanted the reluctant Trevor Brooking to take the job on a permanent basis when he replaced Roeder in a valiant attempt to keep the club in the top flight. But the saintly Brooking had wider ambitions, although nobody really knows what he does at the English FA as the national team disintegrates before our eyes.

The fans deserved a substantial figure to replace Brooking, someone who would get the team back in the Premier League and restore some pride and dignity to the club. The board chose to go for a young manager with a decent track record who might be around for a few years. The board went for Alan Pardew, and with a new, ambitious young manager at the helm, the fans the fans had something to get excited about. The Hammers returned to the Premier League in the new boss's second season in charge, and Bubbles were blowing once again at Upton Park.

Most Hammers' supporters would have settled for a ninth-place finish in the first season after promotion, especially when they were everyone's favourites to go down. To be back at the Millennium Stadium for the third time within 12 months – this time in the FA Cup Final – would have been beyond the wildest dreams of even the most optimistic of supporters.

The first thing on Pardew's mind as the 2005–06 season kicked-off was to preserve their new status alongside the elite clubs in the top flight of English football. Relegation was unthinkable. By the end of the season, with their place in the Premier League assured, West Ham found themselves at Wembley. Well, not actually Wembley, although the 2006 FA Cup Final was the planned opener for the new stadium. The new Wembley was only half-built, had no pitch and was already millions of pounds over budget, so the FA went cap-in-hand to their Welsh counterparts, who agreed to extend the Millennium Stadium agreement. If the wonderful Cardiff ground had not been available, the FA had apparently lined up pitch number 73 on Hackney Marshes as the venue for the 2006 FA Cup Final.

Pardew's squad had been strengthened by the arrival of Teddy Sheringham, Carl Fletcher, Lionel Scaloni, Yossi Benayoun and Dean Ashton, all of whom played significant parts in the unfolding drama of 2006. The only player who would have played but didn't was midfielder Hayden Mullins. The midfielder was suspended after being sent-off in a League game against Liverpool earlier in April. The incident added some spice to the match at Cardiff. Luis Garcia effectively got Mullins sent off in the League game and received a red card himself when the referee's assistant intervened. Both players missed the Final.

The Hammers had a tricky route to Cardiff. Goals from Mullins and Zamora in a 2–1 home win against Norwich City got their Cup run started. The fourth round brought tough opponents to the Boleyn in Premier League side Blackburn Rovers, but the Hammers were in vintage form that day and ran out winners four goals to one, with Sheringham, Etherington and Zamora all on the scoresheet. In the fifth round the Hammers drew another Premier League side in Bolton Wanderers. The tie went into a replay following a 0–0 draw a Bolton, and a spine-tingling match at Upton Park saw the Hammers prevail 2–1 thanks to Harewood's 96th-minute winner.

The sixth round was a personal triumph for Dean Ashton, whose two goals ensured another 2–1 victory and a place in the semi-finals. Ashton was a wonderful centre-forward, certainly the best at the club since Geoff Hurst, which is high praise indeed. He had everything – pace, an excellent first touch, strength in possession and was a brilliant finisher. He could have been the West Ham and England centre-forward for years, but his career was tragically cut short by a series of crippling injuries. We will never know what Dean Ashton might have achieved in the game, and it was a very sad day at Upton Park when he announced his forced retirement.

Liverpool, Chelsea and Middlesborough were with the Hammers in the semi-final draw. For the first time in their excellent Cup run the Hammers fans could dream of the Final. They managed to avoid the big two and travelled to Villa Park to play Middlesborough with their hopes sky high. Nobody wants to lose a semi-final, and the match was a tense affair with both teams well below their best. With extra-time looking the most likely outcome, the hero-of-the-day, Marlon Harewood, stepped in with a late goal to put the Hammers through to the Final and their fans into dreamland.

In the battle of the giants at Old Trafford, Liverpool beat bitter rivals Chelsea 2–1. Everyone in football, with the exception of a few thousand die-hard fans in the East

End of London, believed the Merseysiders were nailed-on favourites to lift the trophy. This didn't concern Alan Pardew and his men, who did well to finish in the top-half of the Premier League. The Cup Final was a real icing-on-the-cake both for the fans and players. But this team knew they had a chance, a slim chance, to put themselves in Hammers' history by winning the club's first trophy since the team of 1980 beat Arsenal at Wembley 1–0. Pardew made sure they knew of their lineage.

On Cup Final day the Cardiff train from Paddington was bang on time and filled to the brim with West Ham supporters heading for the Millennium Stadium. The mood of the fans was restrained, with just the odd self-deprecating remark intended to reduce the tension. There was no singing of Bubbles or chanting legendary names. Everyone was surprisingly subdued. The mood changed dramatically once fans arrived at Cardiff station and had their first glimpse of the stadium.

As supporters left the train they noticed all the streets around the ground were full of other Hammers supporters. The place was a sea of claret and blue. The infamous Scousers were on the other side of the ground – a brilliant piece of stadium design totally separated the two sets of supporters from each other, with different entrances, car parks and station platforms enforcing total segregation. This meant the fans could relax, enjoy the moment and take in the pre-match atmosphere. By the time they took their seats in the West Ham end of this wonderful stadium, the Irons supporters were in full voice and determined to enjoy every single minute of their day in Cardiff.

An hour before kick-off some fans, the author included, experienced one of those 'What have we done?' moments. They discovered that their seats were in the Liverpool end of the ground. There was nothing else to do but work their way through thousands of tightly packed, red-clad Scousers to their gate entrance and try to swap their tickets. The task was made more difficult because they were dressed head-to-toe in claret and blue. The tickets were a prize in a County FA raffle, and the group had no idea they were for the Liverpool end until they arrived at the ground.

Suddenly, right outside their turnstile, several menacing-looking Liverpool supporters surrounded the group, and to their great relief asked if they wanted to swap tickets. Apparently, the Liverpool fans had won theirs in an identical FA raffle. Convinced by a couple of stewards that their tickets were genuine, they completed the exchange and made their way back to the Hammers end of the ground just a few minutes before the teams came out.

When the players entered the arena, the roar from 72,000 fans was ear-shattering. For Alan Pardew leading his team out, it was the highlight of his short managerial career. Rafael Benitez, in his second year in charge at Anfield, had not yet won a domestic trophy.

Liverpool had previously won the FA Cup six times, while the Hammers had chalked up wins in 1964, 1975 and 1980. In a telling statistic of the difference between the two clubs, Liverpool had won the cup four times since Billy Bonds had lifted the trophy in

1980, but for Hammers supporters all that mattered was they were back in the FA Cup Final for the first time in 26 years, and they were going to enjoy their day.

Pardew left Sheringham and Zamora on the bench, and the sight of Gerrard, Alonso, Kewell and Case in the Liverpool midfield reminded supporter what the team was up against. In the first half West Ham attacked the goal at the Liverpool end, and what happened in the first 30 minutes of the match stunned the Reds fans into silence and sent the Irons into paradise.

On 20 minutes Ashton sent a delicious pass through to Scaloni, racing down the right wing. The Argentinian full-back's superb cross into the six-yard box was deflected into his own net by the hapless prince of Scousers, Jamie Carragher. The West Ham end of the stadium erupted, and for the next few minutes the sound of Bubbles echoed around the ground as the Hammers' fans celebrated in style.

Seven minutes later the excitement reached fever-pitch as West Ham scored again. Matthew Etherington, enjoying himself against Carragher, teased the full-back once more before half hitting his shot at Reina in the Liverpool goal. Inexplicably, Reina spilt the ball into the path of the onrushing Ashton, who clipped it into the net to put West Ham 2–0 up after just 28 minutes. All around, fans were dancing and hugging each other in disbelief.

At this stage of the game the Hammers were well on top and looking for a third, but everyone knew Liverpool would fight back. Sure enough, in the 32nd minute Alonso's chip to the far post eluded Scaloni, and Cissé smashed a volley from eight yards past Shaka Hislop. The Hammers went in for the interval a goal up, with their fans cursing Scaloni's error, but the 45 minutes was hugely entertaining and a tribute to the positive attitude of both sides.

The second half got under way with the tension rising at the West Ham end. The Hammers' fans have learnt to be a cautious bunch, and nobody was talking about victory. Then, within a couple of minutes of the restart, right in front of their fans, both Benayoun and Harewood were denied the opportunity to put their side into an unassailable lead. An incredible double save from Reina kept his side in the game. The Hammers paid the price for their misses when, nine minutes later, the freaky Crouch got his head to an Alonso free-kick. The rebound dropped into the path of the unmarked Gerrard, who smashed his shot past Hislop to level the scores.

The two-goal lead was gone and the joy of the first half a distant memory as Liverpool gained the upper hand. For the first time that afternoon we could hear the Reds fans singing. But despite losing their lead, the Hammers refused to capitulate and lose their grip on the trophy. Unbelievably, just at the point when the Liverpool fans were waiting for their team's inevitable victory, West Ham scored a third.

In the 63rd minute Paul Konchesky overlapped powerfully on the left before sending a speculative cross towards Harewood at the far post. The ball never reached the centre-forward but instead drifted over the stranded Reina and nestled into the back of the Liverpool net. With his team back in front, Pardew replaced the injured Dean Ashton with Bobby Zamora, a clear indication of his attacking intentions.

The West Ham fans roared their team on to the victory that was there for the taking. Liverpool were visibly shaken. A few minutes from the end of full-time, fans could clearly see FA officials attach claret-and-blue ribbons to the Cup. Then, in a moment of pure confusion, the fourth official raised his board to reveal he had given Liverpool a four-minute reprieve. At all sides of the ground nerve ends were raw and exposed as the match went into added time. Just a few minutes stood between West Ham and glory.

With one minute remaining Scaloni spotted Cissé lying injured and booted the ball out of play. When the ball was returned to the full-back, instead of launching the ball up the field as far possible, he drifted a pass in the direction of Sheringham. In that single moment West Ham lost the cup. Scaloni's pass was intercepted and knocked across to the Liverpool skipper, lurking unmarked 30 yards out. As a Hammers supporter, the last person you want with the ball 30 yards from goal when you are one minute from victory is Steven Gerrard. The England star cracked a rocket right-foot of a volley low inside Hislop's right-hand post to send the game into extra-time. In that same moment he broke the hearts of the Hammers' fans.

The West Ham players had given everything and had the prize snatched from them in the 94th minute. Their supporters had been hit hard by Gerrard's devastating blow, and hundreds of them sat deflated and disbelieving in their seats, while others, heads in their hands, sobbed their hearts out.

Thirty minutes of extra-time meant that the 2006 FA Cup Final was still up for grabs. But Liverpool had gained the momentum with their captain's late goal. Both teams had made all their substitutions – the Reds had brought on Morientes and Kromkamp, while the Hammers had taken off the stricken Ashton, Carl Fletcher and, surprisingly, Matthew Etherington for Dailly, Zamora and Sheringham.

Players on both sides were suffering from cramp and minor injuries. Marlon Harewood needed extensive treatment for a foot injury and had no choice but to hobble around for the rest of the game. Extra-time was uneventful as neither side committed themselves to all-out attack.

Then, in the 120th minute, the Hammers looked to have won the match all over again. Skipper Reo-Coker deflected a free-kick from deep in the Liverpool half, and, with a goal looking certain, Reina stretched and touched the ball onto the far post. Hyypia failed to make the clearance and the ball fell to Harewood just a few yards from the Hammers' supporters. With the goal and the FA Cup at his mercy, the centre-forward got his injured left foot to the ball but failed to make real contact. The ball spun wide and a golden chance was lost.

West Ham were denied victory in the last minute for the second time in the match, and the Final went into a penalty shoot-out. It was all over in a moment. Reina, who was at fault with two goals, suddenly found his form. His save from Anton Ferdinand's nervously struck penalty clinched the FA Cup for Liverpool for the seventh time in their history. The Hammers had lost the Final 3–1 on penalties.

The mood at the West Ham end of the ground was desolate. Thousands of emotionally drained fans sat distraught and unable to move. Gradually people began to comfort one another and slowly make their way back to their trains and coaches to face the long journey home. The atmosphere in the train was wretched, the complete opposite to the joyous scenes some remembered from Wembley in 1980. But the fans were proud of their team. There was talk of ifs and buts – what might have happened if Dean Ashton had been fully fit and played the whole game? How did Harewood miss an open goal in the final minute of extra-time? As the train approached Paddington the mood lightened a little when we realised the Hammers had been part of what the BBC's John Motson described as 'the greatest FA Cup Final of all time'. West Ham were back in the big time – even if on this occasion they were runners-up. They had every reason to be proud of being a West Ham supporter.

**Final score: West Ham United 3 Liverpool 3**
After penalties West Ham United 1 Liverpool 3
West Ham United: Hislop, Scaloni, Ferdinand, Gabbidon, Konchesky, Benayoun, Reo-Coker, Fletcher (Dailly 77), Etherington (Sheringham 85), Ashton (Zamora 71), Harewood.
Substitutes: Dailly (for Fletcher, 77), Sheringham (for Etherington, 85), Zamora (for Ashton, 71).

# 29.

# WEST HAM UNITED V MANCHESTER UNITED

## PREMIER LEAGUE                    13 MAY 2007

With an FA Cup Final appearance and a ninth-place finish in the Premier League, Alan Pardew made a good start to his tough new job. But what happened in 2006–07 was staggering, even by the recent standards of this crazy football club.

The new season started with the arrival of the sensational pair of Argentinians, Carlos Tevez and Javier Mascherano. The fans could not quite believe their eyes. West Ham had joined the Big Four spending riot. How could this happen? The answer was that West Ham United had been acquired with someone else's money by a biscuit billionaire from Iceland. New owner Magnusson had convinced the gullible board and the club's bankers that he had a few bob and really cared about the future of the club. The truth was that he landed his millions pounds of debt on this sad little club. In a moment of immense hubris, the wannabe Abramovich set out to build a claret-and-blue fantasy team that could carry off the Premier League.

What happened was a train smash of staggering proportions. Within a couple of years the credit crunch exposed the Icelandic economy as a joke, leading Magnusson to sell the club to a consortium of leverage city boys. The financial fiasco ended when of a couple of sharp East Enders bought the club. The pair, Gold and Sullivan, made their fortune on 'light adult entertainment'. The new owners are sharp business people and will take no prisoners, and the fans are happy to get some stability back to their club. The new managing director, Karen Brady, has an eye for detail. Within a week of taking up her new post, she discovered the club had 105 mobile phone contracts at their training ground alone.

In the meantime Pardew was left on his own to cope with two huge Argentinian egos and the loss of his best player, Dean Ashton, for most of the season. By early December the club had been eliminated from the UEFA Cup at the first hurdle, knocked out of the League Cup in the first round and won just four games out of 17.

True to form, the new board panicked and summarily sacked the man who led his team to near-FA Cup triumph and promotion to the Premier League in two seasons. Pardew was sacrificed on the altar of dodgy money and corruption. With Pardew gone, the club pleaded with Charlton to release ex-Hammer Alan Curbishley with the aim of salvaging something from a desperately disappointing season.

Curbishley had done a great job in his six years at Charlton and was a highly respected former Hammer. He had made 85 appearances for West Ham between 1975 and 1979, when he was competing for a midfield place with Brooking, Devonshire, Bonds and Geoff Pike. The former England Under-21 international was one of five children born to a family of dockers in Forest Gate. The fans, despite his success, never really took to Pardew, but were happy with Curbs' appointment, although why he would want the job only he knows.

With relegation looking a certainty, Curbishley led his team to seven wins in the last nine games to keep the club in the Premier League. What of the two saviours from Argentina? Incredibly, given what we have seen since, Mascherano hardly played a game in the 2006–07 season, and his fellow countryman Tevez only came good in the last few games. Most of their non-appearances were because the club had not actually bought the two World Cup stars from their clubs but from some seedy foreign agent. Apparently the contracts were signed in a greasy-spoon 'caff' at the back of Stratford station. Subsequently West Ham were fined for fielding illegally registered players but not deducted any points. This led relegated Sheffield United to sue the Hammers for £30 million for loss of earnings, payable in monthly installments of 10 quid over the next thousand years. Welcome to West Ham United, Curbs!

The ex-midfielder was a good man and decent manager. He was old school and hated the Baby Bentleys and astronomical wages of Premier League players. But, despite the club drowning in debt, Curbishley brought in Lucas Neill and Matthew Upson to shore up the defence, while Reo-Coker, Noble and Bobby Zamora began to settle into the side.

Curbishley got his team into a position where they could mathematically survive, but with the final fixture against Manchester United at Old Trafford, their position looked desperate. Cue Carlos Tevez. The quicksilver striker had won over the North Bank with his passion, endless running and relegation-saving goals. Tevez is one of the very few ex-Hammers who receives a standing ovation when he returns to Upton Park. His name in Hammer history is assured.

The odds on beating Manchester United in front of 75,000 at Old Trafford were marginally improved by the Reds having already beaten Chelsea to the Premiership title. This was offset by the title-holders showing off their new silverware in front of their adoring fans, and happy to see their last opponents of the season disappearing through the Premier League trap-door. But with six wins out of eight behind them, the Londoners arrived in a hopeful mood. They were three points ahead of Wigan in 18th spot, who were facing 16th-place Sheffield United at Bramall Lane.

The Hammers needed a small miracle on 'Survival Sunday' if they were to avoid a repeat of 2003, when relegation led to the mass exodus of the best group of youngsters ever assembled at the club. Just a single point might have been enough, but a defeat seemed the likeliest outcome and then a wait to see what happened elsewhere. If the Hammers notched up three points at Old Trafford then Sheffield United would need to beat Wigan to stay up.

The Manchester match had added spice because West Ham had beaten Alex Ferguson's side at Upton Park earlier in the season in Curbishley's first game in charge. Shock results are not supposed to happen to the genial Scot's team. A double over Manchester United would have been the shock of the Premier League season.

Before the kick-off, the West Ham players formed a guard of honour to welcome the new champions onto the pitch. Within a few minutes of the start, Wayne Rooney hit a stunning drive just over the bar, and minutes later Benayoun cleared off the line from both Kieran Richardson and Alan Smith. Then, with the Hammers fans' nerves now fully exposed, the news came through from Bramall Lane that Wigan had gone a goal up, which sent Sheffield United into the bottom three. The permutations were bewildering and most fans tried to forget them and concentrate on the match.

The Hammers fans in the ludicrously named Theatre of Dreams were about to witness their best moment since they led Liverpool 2–0 in the 2006 FA Cup Final the previous season. In a never-forgotten moment, Robert Green sent a long down-field clearance deep into the Reds' half. Zamora got his head to it first and deflected the ball into the path of Carlos Tevez. The two strikers played a neat one-two before Tevez eluded Wes Brown and dinked the ball from the narrowest of angles past the advancing Van der Sar into the net. Tevez had gone from zero to hero at West Ham in less than a few weeks, and his goal that day had given the Hammers a slim chance of survival. You could sense the relief among the West Ham supporters as Bubbles rang round Old Trafford. For the rest of the match, the Reds' fortress felt like home game for the travelling Hammers fans, while the home crowd was stunned into an uncomfortable silence.

Early in the second half supporters heard that Wigan had scored again, making Sheffield United favourites for the drop. The Hammers began the second period defending deep in the own half, and they succeeded in containing the dangerous Smith before Ferguson introduced substitutes Ryan Giggs, Paul Scholes and Christiano Ronaldo into the action in a desperate late bid to end their season in style.

West Ham fans had little time to ponder on the luxury of having this kind of talent on the substitutes' bench when John O'Shea had a penalty appeal turned down. In the frantic last phase of the game, the Hammers hung on by the skin of their teeth. In the dying minutes Rob Green produced an amazing acrobatic save to deny Scholes an equaliser, and he confirmed his England potential with an excellent stop from a powerful Ronaldo header in the dying minutes.

With Mullins on for the tiring Tevez and Harewood replacing Zamora, the visitors managed to hold out until referee Atkinson finally blew for time. The Hammers, with a backs-to-the-wall display against the might of Manchester United, had secured their Premier League place for another season and in the process sent down a bitterly disappointed Sheffield United. The Old Trafford faithful watched in disbelief as the away supporters celebrated their team's victory. Sir Alex was presented with the Premier League trophy at the end of the game, but miraculously West Ham had stolen the show.

The Hammers' great escape had seem unlikely in March, when they were 10 points adrift and Tevez's shooting boots were lost somewhere in South America. Alan Pardew had Mascherano and Tevez forced on him, but it was Curbishley who profited from Tevez's timely, late-season goal burst.

Mark Noble was many fans' Man of the Match that day, confirming his immense promise. Reo-Coker was everywhere, while Collins, skipper Neill and the brilliant Robert Green played heroically against one of the best attacking sides in Europe.

With their Premier League future secure, at least for a season, West Ham could look forward with a little more optimism than usual. However, the habitual crazy, agent-driven pre-season transfer fest saw Reo-Coker, Harewood, Zamora and Benayoun replaced with varying success by Matthew Upson, Robert Parker, John Pantsil, Carlton Cole, Kieran Dyer, Craig Bellamy, Freddie Ljungberg and Nolberto Solano. The new season also brought a new manager.

**Final score: Manchester United 0 West Ham United 1**
West Ham United: Green, Neill, Collins, Ferdinand, McCartney, Benayoun, Reo-Coker, Noble, Boa Morte, Zamora, Tevez, Spector, Harewood, Mullins.

# 30.

# WEST HAM UNITED V BLACKBURN ROVERS

## PREMIER LEAGUE                    30 AUGUST 2008

2007–08 was a good season for West Ham fans, despite losing heavily to Chelsea, Tottenham and Liverpool in their first three games. But Curbishley's fortunes turned with a 4–1 win at home against Blackburn Rovers, which included a goal from the teenage goalscoring sensation Freddie Sears. The young striker joined Mark Noble from the Academy in the true traditions of West Ham. With youngsters like James Tomkins, Zavon Hines, and Jack Collison joining Noble and Sears, the club had the best crop of youngsters since the Joe Cole/Michael Carrick generation a few years earlier.

The team was delighted to finish their campaign in 10th position, three points ahead of London rivals Spurs, despite losing top signings Bellamy and Dyer for almost the whole season. The West Ham faithful were relieved not to have yet another relegation battle to ruin their winter, and this modest improvement on the previous year was the least the fans expected.

On the pitch at least, the club appeared settled, and if Curbishley could get all his players fit the future looked reasonably assured. The bizarre Argentinian episode was behind them, although the ownership of the Irons was approaching farcical proportions as the debts mounted to a terrifying £50 million. There were serious concerns for the future of the club as the bankers began to close in. But somehow the club survived and the fans, as ever, remained loyal, although their patience was tested to the full throughout this period.

A match against Blackburn Rovers at the start of the 2008–09 season may appear a strange choice, but the match had real significance for West Ham United. The club made the belated decision to officially withdraw the number-six shirt, traditionally associated with the greatest player in the club's history, Bobby Moore. With Philip Jackson's wonderful statues of Moore at Wembley Stadium and Upton Park and the renaming of the South Bank, the club had at last fully acknowledged their debt to its local hero, one of the greatest players ever to have graced the game of football.

It is difficult to understate the importance of the name of Bobby Moore to West Ham United and the pride the fans feel in his achievements. To have a permanent tribute to Moore at the Boleyn acts as a reminder of the club's proud past, while retiring his number-six shirt is a symbolic act of respect that assures the continuance of his reputation at the club in perpetuity. The shirt was actually withdrawn at half-time in a pre-season friendly at Upton Park against Spain's Villarreal. The occasion was the new Bobby Moore Cup, and Moore's shirt was surrendered at half-time by Matthew Upson, who played the remainder of the match in his squad number, number 15.

In a corner of the ground at every home game a giant screen carries a picture of Moore in his number-six shirt. The image is the logo of the Bobby Moore Fund, a cancer charity established by Moore's widow, Stephanie. The Fund has raised millions of pounds for cancer research, and Stephanie and her team work tirelessly to educate the public to the dangers of bowel cancer. In August 2008 the club had at last made its peace with its greatest son, but in a curious way the gesture seemed like a break with the past rather than a remembrance of a glorious era. Fans will hope that retiring the great man's shirt did not signal the end of West Ham United as one of the most creative forces in English football.

The first home game of the new season brought Blackburn Rovers to Upton Park. Rovers were managed by the self-styled Guv'nor of Premier League football, former Hammer Paul Ince. The ex-Manchester United star and former England captain was detested by Hammers' supporters, who have never forgiven their local boy for flirting publicly with the Reds while still a West Ham player. The home fans would have been able to compare the shoddy behaviour of Ince with the dignified, almost saintly conduct of Bobby Moore.

The Blackburn match was also significant because in the Hammers' midfield was the best player seen at the Boleyn for a few seasons, midfielder Scott Parker. A Londoner, Parker was brought in from Newcastle United and had all the qualities Upton Park likes to see in their players – lovely touches, brilliant passes and spectacular goals. On top of this Parker had a heart as big as the pitch. Here was a player in the club's finest traditions of midfield magic – and he was local. Parker was over the injury problems that had held up his career, and with a couple of seasons the future of the club appeared to hinge on keeping him.

In the side with Parker was Dean Ashton, who had only a handful of games ahead of him before his tragic premature retirement. The Hammers quickly went two up though a Davenport header and an own-goal by Blackburn defender Samba. Big Jason Roberts pulled a goal back for the Rovers, easily turning the laughingly slow Davenport before sliding his shot under Robert Green. The Hammers went in for the interval in the lead, having a scored two goals in the first 45 minutes in August – happy days.

The second period began in dramatic fashion when Rovers were gifted a penalty after Carlton Cole tried to practise his basketball skills in the opposition penalty area. Hammer of the Year Rob Green threw himself to his left to produce a spectacular save from Roberts. The Hammers' 'keeper was looking one of the best in the Premier League and was pushing for England selection.

With Blackburn chasing the game in the dying minutes, the Irons scored twice on the counter-attack. Craig Bellamy, on as substitute in his first appearance of the season, volleyed the third, and two minutes later Carlton Cole slid the ball over the line seconds before the referee whistled for time.

The result brought misery for Rovers and their manager but delight for the Hammers as they moved up to fourth spot in the table with six points out of nine. Of course, the fans were not fooled by such early-season false dawns, but they would have been happy their team won on a day when they paid tribute to their saintly old number six.

**Final score: West Ham United 4 Blackburn Rovers 1**
West Ham United: Green, Neill, Parker, Ashton, Etherington, Cole, Upson, Noble, Faubert, Behrami, Davenport, McCartney, Bellamy, Mullins.

Just when everything at West Ham seemed nicely settled for a few seasons, the bunch of incompetents who ran the club pressed the self-destruct button. The board sold Anton Ferdinand and full-back George McCartney, but forgot to mention it to their manager. Not unreasonably, Curbishley went ballistic when he found out. It was the principle that angered him. The players were dispensable, especially the pathetic Anton Ferdinand. He was never as good as his brother, and in mid-season he had lied to his manager about visiting his sick grandmother in the States when he was actually lying on a Barbados beach knocking back the Red Stripe. Ferdinand typified everything about the Premier League that Curbishley detested.

The manager resigned immediately over the sale of his players and refused to reconsider. On 3 September, the start of the 2008–09 season, West Ham were again searching for a new manager. The board wasted no time in bringing in the legendary Italian striker Gianfranco Zola, whose only managerial experience was a few games leading the Italian Under-21 side. The Hammers were one point away from the relegation zone at Christmas but recovered to finish ninth, just missing out on European qualification. The 12th manager in the club's history enjoyed an impressive second half of the season, despite the boardroom battles that were unsettling to everyone at the club.

# THEY FLY SO HIGH...

The Hammers were relegated from the Premiership in 2003 but were up again in 2005, the year they met Liverpool in the FA Cup Final. In the years between 1988 and 2005 West Ham were relegated four times and promoted on three occasions. Managers have come and gone. Bonds, Redknapp, Macari, Roeder and Curbishley all failed to bring the best out of generations of wonderfully talented young players.

Since the Fenton/Greenwood/Lyall era the club has rather lost its way, and even the most die-hard supporters would probably admit to each other that the Hammers' enviable reputation for attacking, free-flowing football is at risk. The traditional family ownership of the club has gone the way of the others in the Premier League. Financial leverage, consortium ownership and debt-refinancing are the new buzz-words uttered, usually by foreign owners keen to use high-profile football clubs to promote their main business interests.

Continued questions about the club's finances have taken their toll on successive managers and their players. The Boleyn ground has been improved, although the old Chicken Run is now well past its sell-by date. The new owners are in discussions with Newham Council about moving to the new Olympic Stadium in Stratford. The fans hate the idea as much as the Bonds Scheme introduced by the club in 1992. One fan expressed his feelings on a club forum: 'Upton Park is in our blood.' Another spoke for many when he said, 'The Hammers will never compete with the Big Four, we are what we are and we love it that way.' Memorable matches are what the West Ham fans want, not brand-new cavernous, glitzy stadiums shared with athletics and goodness knows what else. But perhaps the supporters need to change their outlook to match the ambitions of Green Street-born chairman David Gold – perhaps the Olympic Stadium is the future for West Ham United.

When Gianfranco Zola was appointed manager in 2008, the club looked set for a bright new era at Upton Park, following a 10th-place finish in the Premier League. However, Zola's team struggled in 2009 and narrowly missed relegation, and the Italian was sacked. The bright new era lasted just one season.

The future of West Ham United lies in the club's admired youth policy. The commitment to youngsters remains with Tomkins, Collison, Nouble and Sears joining Mark Noble from the Chadwell Heath Academy. The fans hope that these new young stars will not go the same way as Ferdinand, Cole and Carrick.

As we look forward to the 2010–11 season with a new manager in Avram Grant, only Mark Noble remains at the club from the team of 2005. The young lad from Canning Town is West Ham through-and-through and, to the amusement of the team's foreign players, sings Bubble at the top of his voice in the tunnel before games. He has made a promising start to his career with a hatful of England Under-

21 appearances, and a full cap cannot be far away for the young midfielder, who has been known to walk home from the ground after a home match. At the age of 23 Noble is the longest serving player at Upton Park, and all fans hope that he will be the heart of the team for many years to come. Potentially he is in the Moore/Brooking/Bonds category, and the fans are desperate for him to stay at Upton Park.

A club like West Ham is rooted in its past, and a strong bond has always existed between the players and supporters. The fans know their history. They understand that their predecessors worked and played football for the Thames Ironworks in the East London Docks. They are extremely proud that West Ham United provided three players – Moore, Hurst and Peters – for England's only World Cup-winning side. This rare feat is unlikely to recur given the current number of foreign players in the line ups of most Premier League teams.

Three FA Cup Final victories and a European Cup triumph in a 100-year history is a modest haul and cannot compare with the achievements of the Hammers' more illustrious rivals. This won't matter a jot to the fans, who remain proud of their club, which, since the days of founder Arnold Hills, has remained committed to football's highest ideals. Local lads playing exciting, free-flowing, attacking football against good opposition are the ingredients for memorable matches involving West Ham United, win, lose or draw. Long may they continue. Up the Hammers!